The Alien Chronicles

The Alien Chronicles

Compelling Evidence For UFOs & Extraterrestrial Encounters
In Art & Texts Since Ancient Times

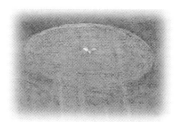

MATTHEW HURLEY

Edited by Neil Hague

Quester

First published in 2003 by
Quester Publications
PO Box 3226
Chester
CH4 7ZB
United Kingdom

Cover Painting
The Baptism of Christ by Aert De Gelder (1710)
© Courtesy of the Fitzwilliam Museum Cambridge
Design: Mark Gouldthorpe at *Silver Monkey*
Typography: Carl Bowes
Picture Editor: Neil Hague
Proof Reading: Sally McCulloch

Printed and bound by Regal of Hong Kong

British Library Cataloguing-in Publication Data
A catalogue record for this book is
available from the British Library

ISBN 0-9541904-1-6

ACKNOWLEDGEMENTS
ACKNOWLEDGEMENTS

I would like to thank a number of people for making this book happen: Firstly, Frank Segler for his generosity in making this project a reality, Neil Hague for taking the project on board and his guidance, David Maclaren for revamping my website, Bob Dean for the inspiration, Alain Stauffer, Anne and Whitley Strieber (*www.unknowncountry.com*), Barry Chamish, Bill Chalker, Chris Aubeck, Comic Court, Deril Sims, Peter Sorenson, Phil Hoyle, Ulrich Dopatka, Erich Von Däniken, (*www.daniken.com*), Christian Frehner, Billy Meier, Eric Oscar, Ernie Vega, Ian Dubin, Isabella Dusi, Scott Klinger, Joe Rogerio, Dominqiue Lemaire, Marco Gee, Mirko (*www.mmmgroup*), Ole John Braenne, Raymond Fowler, Graham Birdsall, Russell Callaghan, Allen Roberts, Robert S Digby, Rudolf Bosnjak, Stephane Bernard, Daniela Giordano, Galen R Frysinger, Gary Anthony, Paul Tucker, Natalie Broulliette. There are of course many others whose names escape me but you know who you are!

I wish to acknowledge all of the authors whose works have been briefly quoted or referred to in the text and in the notes and references. If I have inadvertently overlooked anyone I hope I will have used their work appropriately and that they will accept my thanks.

To
Mum & Dad

CONTENTS

*"All this visible universe is not unique in nature,
and we must believe that there are in other regions of space,
other worlds, other beings and other men."*

Lucretius, 99-55 BC

PREFACE

PREFACE
PREFACE

What if everything you thought about UFOs was wrong? What would it mean if there were an irrefutable historical record of UFOs that appeared in every age of human existence and in every culture? In prehistoric cave dwellings, man recorded what he saw in the world around him by carefully painting these things on cave walls. As soon as mankind was creating art chiselled into stone, so too does there appear UFOs. In paintings from the Middle Ages down to the Renaissance, there seems to appear unmistakable evidence that this phenomenon was appearing on a regular basis. And no sooner had photography been invented then UFOs continued to show up over cities and in the countryside accross every part of the globe. All of this evidence will appear in the following pages.

It is commonly thought that UFO sightings started during (or right after) World War II. During World War II there were many sightings of 'foo fighters'. In 1947 Kenneth Arnold, in his now famous sighting over Washington's Cascade Mountains, observed objects which were subsequently christened 'flying saucers'. But this story does not start in 1947.

What you will see put forth in this book is nothing short of a major revolution in how we view the world around us. This comprehensive collection of documentary evidence begs for answers. Indeed it begs the original questions. What in the world are these things that have appeared throughout the ages. In wonderment man has looked to the heavens and while grasping at whatever explanation their time period would permit, was good enough to record these events for us. And now this package, this set of facts is dropped into our laps and defies common explanation.

UFOs and related phenomenon have a real history all of there own and this history is woven among and just below the surface of the history that we are all familiar with. It is so pervasive that it covers nearly all time periods, all cultures and all of the inhabited continents! This book challenges our very concept of an orderly progression of history. It shows the impossible. And yet it is true, with names and places of these works of art duly recorded for all to reference.

PRIMITIVE VIEWS

To appreciate the full impact that a sighting of these strange events would have had on say a 12th Century witness; you need to understand their frame of mind. They would never have seen a flying object of any sort. Considering that no ordinary human was capable of flight, or of being behind these strange aerial sights, they could only have assumed that these sightings were supernatural in origin, and imbued with theological meaning. All that was unexplained and unexplainable was the providence of God.

There is a very subtle filter, a linguistic distorter whereby and how various cultures interpret their surroundings. This alters meaning over time. As an example, in today's modern world, the symbols in Chinese for 'computer' are actually written down as lightning (as one symbol) and brain (as the second symbol). In this example you can see ancient meaning being applied to describe a modern technology. If we came across say the Egyptian equivalent of 'lightning brain', how would we interpret this? I think it would be very difficult for the reader thousands of years hence to understand what was really meant. We have lost sight of this historical record because the language used to describe this phenomenon has changed too. We would need to go back and re-interpret much of these olden texts and works and bring them up to date with our more modern understandings of what is possible. The various sciences have generally interpreted ancient texts in a highly esoteric manner, assigning afterlife or supernatural associations to nearly everything. They 'over-interpret' texts, imbuing them with meanings that the original writer might not have intended.

So numerous are these ancient sightings that in the 4th Century BC the historian Obsequens, compiled a detailed and eerily familiar listing of UFOs and unexplained aerial phenomenon. Over and over again the veil of time immemorial is swept aside to reveal that myth is in fact a soberly written account of fact. So too we propose that the works of art contained herein have been accurate representations by persons who were eyewitnesses or who were contemporaries of those who did.

SPECIFIC EXAMPLES

There are many compelling pictures in this volume. One of my favourites is *Glorification of the Eucharist* by Bonaventura Salimbeni (1595). This picture clearly shows a device of technological origin. It even has antenna protruding from the top. Amazingly the orientation of the antenna gives us further proof as to its technical purpose. It is in a classic 'V' or 'rabbit ears', which is the optimal arrangement designed to capture radio waves. There are even 'nubs' at the end of both antennas, which is a classic feature existing on every single antenna currently being produced. There is symmetrical sheathing on both sides about 6 inches from the sphere. They both taper off at the ends, or are wider at the bottom and narrower at the top. Additionally, one can also see grommets, which cinch the protrusions into place, at the base of both antennas. So this object was in fact well-designed and done so to be durable, as evidenced by these fastening grommets.

The incredible level of detail shown in this picture forces me to conclude that the artist had this object first hand and was able to paint in exacting detail what he saw. This so clearly resembles a 20th Century manufactured product that one could be forgiven if they thought that it was a contemporary painting of Sputnik! Except that it is 500 years old!

Finally, if one compares the above mentioned painting *Glorification of the Eucharist* with a work done about 150 years earlier, which appears in the book entitled *Le Livre Des Bonnes Moeurs*, you will see some surprising similarities. Both show orbs, both are aerial phenomenon and both show banding surrounding the object!

Another stunning example is *The Annunciation* by Carlo Crivelli (1486), which shows a directed beam of light travelling quite some distance without diffraction or diffusion. This light beam issues forth from a UFO object in the clouds, and goes straight down to the head of the praying Virgin Mary. Light, like gravity, obeys the inverse square law, which is to say that it diffuses over distance and it weakens as it diffuses. Neither phenomenon is shown in this picture. Therefore, it is impossible for persons who painted this picture (and the many like it) to have directly observed light behaving in this manner. Unless of course you accept the fact that technological means were available hundreds of years before our standard telling of history says it was, and that it was capable of creating collimated light, able to travel great distance without deteriorating the intensity.

In the corner of the Visoki Decani monastery in Kosovo, Yugoslavia, we find a mural of the crucifixion of Christ. Within the painting there seems to be what appear to be aircraft or spacecraft. Each craft has a single figure inside and each one has the occupant with hands forward on what could only be described as handling controls of some sort. The artist, or artists that made this mural seemed to be hinting at an airborne craft, occupied by 'someone', which would give reason for the aerodynamically tapered front and what seems like an exhaust (fire or something) at the rear of the ship!

Contained in this volume are many works of art, spanning the ages that provide unmistakable proof of the existence of UFOs. What these things are, why they are here, if they are a natural phenomenon or otherwise, are all open to debate, interpretation and hopefully scientific inquiry. Our close mindedness has blinded us to huge swaths of our own history and therefore we cannot answer even the simplest questions about the unexplained phenomenon contained herein. However, the answers await us. It is my sincere hope that this book piques our collective curiosity and helps to encourage a real search for the answers. The truth is out there.

Here now, enjoy and prepare to be surprised by the detailed and thorough compilation of the most compelling argument one could make for the existence of UFOs.

Frank Segler

INTRODUCTION

This book is really the culmination of my interest in UFOs, which started as a young child after my imagination was captured watching Spielberg's *Close Encounters of the Third Kind*. From that moment the concept of beings from other planets visiting us was crystallised in my mind. Within all of us there is the capacity to question and ponder the deeper implications in life. I have had this 'mind set' since I was a young child. Maybe the sometimes complex and bizarre world of Ufology was meant for me.

I do not come from any religious background, and, consequently, this has helped me look at Ufology with an open mind and not to be clouded by a narrow outlook. In terms of God, I have always favoured the idea of a pantheistic creator. That is that God is at the core of every atom. This definition was exemplified when I was about seven; in school we were all asked to draw a picture of God, everyone drew an old man with a beard, whereas I just drew a flame. To me the creator was just an impersonal absolute. This 'definition' has repeatedly been mentioned in alleged ET encounters all across the globe.

As a child I can remember visiting the local library scanning the shelves for UFO books. Back then (1981) there was no Internet, no high street UFO magazines. Typically there would just be a handful of books with a few poor black and white photos. I did, however, find these books fascinating and my deep, questioning mind was being fed, like a bee to nectar. I never found the idea of beings from other worlds visiting us strange or odd. Why not? We live in a big universe! People often say the distances are too great for beings to traverse to our planet. But look how much we have advanced in 150 years. We have gone from a horse and cart to a Space Shuttle. Now, consider the idea that there may be races out there that are hundreds, millions or billions of years ahead of us in technology. Surely their mastery of physics and interstellar travel would be mind blowing. Science only knows what it has discovered, not what it has not discovered. As Albert Einstein once said:

"The most beautiful experience we can have is the mysterious. It is the fundamental emotion that stands at the cradle of true art and true science. Whoever does not know it and can no longer wonder, no longer marvel, is as good as dead, and his eyes are dimmed."

Moving on several years my interest in UFOs was now starting to expand. I was becoming increasingly interested in the idea of the existence of the human soul or spirit. Is there an afterlife? Do we reincarnate? My reading matter widened with books on Spiritualism and other related occult subjects. In 1995 I attended a UFO conference in Leeds. What I saw there, during a talk by Ufologist Bob Dean, set the seed for the writing of this book. Bob showed a series of Renaissance paintings featuring flying saucer like objects. My jaw dropped when I saw them and I think everyone else in the lecture hall was captivated as well. What were they doing there? Did the artists see UFOs then? Were the artists inspired? Were they on drugs? Did they have some arcane knowledge about UFOs? It seemed to me that we have a pictorial record of visitation by UFOs going back hundreds of years. I realised this was important material in providing gravitas to the concept that UFOs have been visiting us throughout history. It was now time to initiate my quest into these matters and collate together as much evidence as I could of UFO and possibly ET visitation throughout history.

Moving on into 1997, those images I saw back then, were playing on my mind and I had an intense urge to compile a list of the titles and the artists. I decided to contact Graham Birdsall at *UFO Magazine UK*, informing him I was researching into these old artworks and I asked him if he knew of the paintings Bob Dean showed at the 1995 conference I attended. Graham did not but kindly sent me a copy of *Cosmic Top Secret* - a video of a presentation given by Bob Dean in Leeds in 1996. When I watched this video, Bob showed even more artworks than at the conference I attended. This time I was able to replay the video and make a note of the titles and artists as Bob described them or at least a description of them. Up to this point I had a list of about seven artworks. The next important stage in my research came in 1998 when the now defunct *Live TV* had a series called *The Why Files*. This was a short daily documentary featuring various unexplained paranormal items. One day I happened to watch it and this particular episode featured an elderly English gentleman discussing his research into UFOs and old artworks. He showed some artworks I hadn't seen before. Now my list of old artworks was pushing into double figures and I was beginning to wonder how many there were dotted around in galleries and churches around the world.

Late December 2000 I set up my website entitled *Historical Artwork and UFOs* - a pictorial collection of artworks featuring UFOs. It was an instant hit with the UFO community. Over a two year period I received tens of thousands of visitors. I was interviewed on US radio on three occasions and wrote several magazine articles. People were fascinated by my research and during late 2001 I decided to write this book on the subject of Ufology from an historical perspective, weaving both written and pictorial accounts of UFOs.

The main facet of this book is to draw the reader's attention to the myriad of evidence that has existed for thousands of years for the visitation of UFOs. The evidence leans strongly, I feel, in favour of an ET hypothesis. The book has been split into eight key chapters. Firstly, an overview of contemporary Ufology, which examines the various phenomena under the umbrella of Ufology. Chapter two looks at the art of interpretation, an important skill to possess when looking at any piece of text or artwork. Chapter three consists of a comprehensive summary of creational stories from ancient cultures around the globe. Many of these 'advanced' cultures have accounts of beings coming down from the heavens; some even describe the craft and the noise they made. Are these accounts the work of early creative writers or should they be taken literally? Chapter four looks at examples of prehistoric artwork depicting UFOs, predominately in the form of cave paintings and petroglyphs. As well as what appear to be flying craft this chapter also features photos of many artworks showing strange figures, often hooded or surrounded by a halo, sometimes wearing robes or possessing antennae! Are these depictions of the occupants of these flying vehicles? Chapter five lists all the western religious artworks I have come across, which appear to depict what look like UFOs; many of which have come from medieval tapestries and beautiful Renaissance oil paintings. Next time you study an old painting look carefully in the sky. All these chapters will have comparisons with modern Ufology cases where relevant.

Countless accounts of anomalous structured craft litter old library archives around the world and chapter six details many written accounts of flying craft from before Christ to 1900. From examining this chapter the reader will realise that people have always observed flying objects. A number of these written accounts feature illustrations as well. Like today, some of them will have been natural phenomenon but maybe not all. Chapter seven provides the reader with an extensive examination of what many call 'Out of place artifacts', that is, ancient objects that should not really have existed within their time frame. They exhibit a high degree of technology, sophistication or knowledge that may be the result of extraterrestrial contact. Lastly, chapter eight presents a unique portfolio of the earliest known UFO photographs.

If one is to fully appraise the UFO phenomenon, one needs to travel back through time to the distant past and examine the clues and evidence left behind by the artists and writers of each epoch. Hopefully this introduction has given you an insight into the major sequences of events that has led up to the creation of this book. I hope you enjoy it and marvel at the evidence captured by the various artists, whom without their images, this project would not be possible. Ultimately it is for each and every one of us to make up our own minds on what we read and see.

Matthew Hurley

UFOLOGY TODAY *Chapter One*

Before we step into the past it is useful to have an overview of the state of Ufology today. According to many Ufologists the first sighting of a UFO took place in the United States on the 24th June 1947 by pilot Kenneth Arnold. Arnold was flying his aircraft when he reported sighting nine crescent shaped objects over the Cascade Mountains, Washington. From that day the term 'flying saucer' was born and the world began to recognise this term as meaning Extraterrestrial Spacecraft. A popular idea within Ufology is that ETs started to visit our planet in the 1940s, after being attracted once we started to test Atom bombs; it was theorised that ETs were concerned with the potential damage to the planet and to ourselves. This theory has certain logic and seems a neat conjecture. This book, however, aims to dispel this myth.

When one thinks of the UFO phenomenon one automatically thinks of ETs and little green men. Strictly speaking however, UFO stands for a multitude of things - it is simply a flying object that is unidentified. Repeated analysis of UFO sightings conclude that 95% are explainable, the remaining 5% are unexplainable and possibly ET in origin. People see

Figure 1) An early UFO photograph (below left):
Taken in the city of Tientsin, Hopeh Province, China in 1942. A young Japanese student Masujiro Kiryu, whilst going through his fathers scrapbook of photographs from the China Campaign, just before World War II, discovered a strange cone-shaped object in the sky above a Tientsin Street. A number of people in the street are looking up and two are pointing up at the object. A sidewalk photographer snapped a picture of the strange machine and his father bought it from the street vendor for a souvenir of the place.

© *Courtesy of Mr Wendelle Stevens*

The photograph on the opposite page is of the Galaxy formation crop circle. Courtesy of Peter Sorensen © 2001

UFOs from all walks of life and there are many credible witnesses including pilots, air traffic controllers, policemen and astronauts. Cosmonaut Alexander Baladin stated that 'flying saucers' have come into close proximity to the MIR space station as well as the Baikonur Cosmodrom. He added there is sufficient evidence to warrant a scientific study of the phenomenon, and that it is time that world governments officially acknowledge the UFO phenomenon's existence. Baladin disclosed on the December 23, 1998, at Brazil's First International Ufology Forum, that he and fellow cosmonaut Musa Manarov had seen UFOs. During docking operations between his space capsule and the MIR, Baladin saw a glowing object a short distance away. Manarov managed to capture the strange phenomenon on videotape that was shown during the UFO congress in Brazil. Baladin claimed that the recording and other evidence presented during the Congress: *"...must be studied by an international scientific commission."* Baladin insisted that the Russian military has a great contribution to make to UFO research, giving as an example the multiple-witness case at the Kapustin Yar missile base, whose personnel sighted a semi-circular object flying at low altitude lighting up the base's facilities with a powerful searchlight in June 1989. Baladin said:

"Many of my old comrades, who are now working at top-secret military facilities, acknowledge having seen UFOs."[1]

General Vladimir Ivanov, former commander of Russia's Military Space Forces, recalls that three objects flew at a considerable altitude over Baikonur Cosmodrome and were picked up on radar. *"There is no way they could have been airplanes,"* insisted the cosmonaut.

In the last 10 years we have witnessed an explosion of interest in Ufology, particularly through the media with films like *Independence Day*, *Men in Black* and the ever-popular series *The X-Files*. NASA and the scientific community are actively searching for evidence of extraterrestrial life, but what if we were confronted with undeniable proof that ETs exist and that they have been visiting Earth for thousands of years? A Roper survey was conducted on behalf of the National Institute for Discovery Science (NIDS); a privately funded scientific research organisation based in Las Vegas, NV and gave an interesting insight into the public's position on UFOs. The pollsters asked a nationwide sample of 1,971 men and women a variety of questions concerning a sudden confirmation of extraterrestrial life: When asked what they thought UFOs were, 25% thought they were alien spaceships, 12% thought they were secret government programmes, 9% said hallucinations, 19% said UFOs are normal events that are misinterpreted by witnesses, and 7% said travellers from other dimensions. When asked whom they would choose to make first contact with ETs on Earth, 20% said the military, 29% said scientists, 14% said the government, 11% said religious leaders and 20% said a private organisation that had planned for such a contingency.

ROSWELL

Many people are now familiar with the 'Roswell Incident'. The story goes that a spacecraft crashed in Roswell, New Mexico in July 1947. A local farmer Mac Brazel discovered wreckage, along with several alien bodies. The authorities were quickly on the scene and took the wreckage and cadavers away. Initially the information officer at the 509th Bomb Group at Roswell issued a press release saying that they had recovered a flying disc. This was later changed to a weather balloon. In 1994 the Office of the Secretary of the Air Force conducted an exhaustive search for records in response to a General Accounting Office (GAO) inquiry of the incident. The focus of the GAO probe, initiated at the request of a member of Congress, was to determine if the US Air Force, or any other US government agency, possessed information on the alleged crash and recovery of an extraterrestrial vehicle and its alien occupants near Roswell, N.M. in July 1947. The 1994 Air Force report concluded that the predecessor to the US Air Force, the US Army Air Forces, recovered debris from an Army Air Forces balloon-borne research project code named MOGUL. Records located describing research carried out under the MOGUL project; most of which were never classified (and publicly available) were collected, provided to GAO, and published in one volume for ease of access for the general public. The 'aliens' observed in the New Mexico desert were actually anthropomorphic test dummies that were carried aloft by US Air Force high altitude balloons for scientific research. Despite this statement, ET enthusiasts were not persuaded and pointed to the fact the many witnesses who have gone on the record over the years stated they saw non-human cadavers which remarkably resemble what many in Ufology would call a 'Grey alien'. Others have stated they saw or handled metallic fragments from the wreckage, which possessed strange properties, in that it was unusually light and could not be cut or burned.

As time passes it appears that UFOs and the ETs enter more and more into the vocabulary of people. In some ways it doesn't matter if officially they do not exist. ETs & UFOs today are part of our culture. The Internet reflects this fact and is teaming with sites devoted to the subject. In fact it is one of the most popular subjects on the Internet. Intriguing objects are being caught on camcorder around world. Officials from various government and military organisations are stepping forward and imparting their experiences. This has been matched by a large increase in sightings.

Various 'UFO hotspots' have sprung up around the world also. Arguably the most prolific are in Mexico. Since 1991 there has been an explosion of UFO sightings and excited locals and media have shot many hours of video footage depicting disc shaped craft flying around sometimes in large clusters. They appear to be metallic with no visible means of propulsion. Interestingly, the Mayans predicted the dawning of the Sixth Sun (another name for the new age on Earth) would start after the solar eclipse on July 11th 1991.[2]

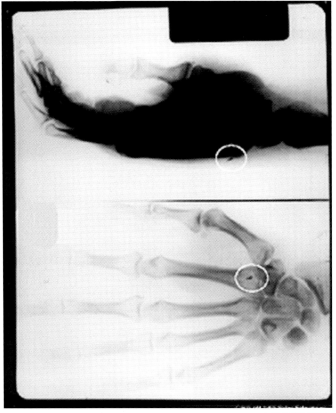

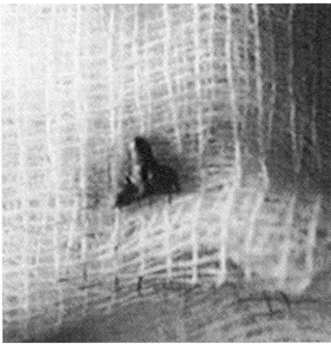

ALIEN ABDUCTION

Another phenomenon under the umbrella of Ufology that has come to the fore in the last few decades is that of Alien Abduction. Individuals through hypnosis, although sometimes consciously as well, report being taken on board a craft and examined by strange beings. They are normally described as being about 4ft tall, greyish skin, oversized heads with large black wrap around eyes. There is often a taller figure that appears to be in command. This can be a taller 'Grey' or an Insectoidal like figure. Medical proceedures usually take place and occasionally there is communication between both parties. Abductees often recall abduction events stemming back to early childhood. It therefore appears to researchers that the individual experiences repeated abductions throughout their life and are somehow 'tagged'.

Figure 2) An X-ray of an implant from an 'abductee'. (above left)
(Below left): The removed implant.
In 1995, UFO investigator Derrel Sims coordinated the first surgeries in a controlled and documented setting to remove alleged alien implants. The first two patients (one of whose x-ray appears on the left) had experienced apparent alien abduction. Though the two patients had never met, anecdotal similarities involving their reported experiences and the behavior of their implants existed between them — and their excised objects were identical. The pathology, as Sims had specifically predicted, was highly unusual. Blind tests done on the two metal 'T' shaped objects revealed extraterrestrial properties, similar to what would appear in a very rare meteor formation. Sims initial discovery of the alleged implanted/embedded objects phe-

nomena resulted from his own conscious experience in 1960 at the age of twelve. This event forever changed his worldview and gave him the clues in his search for physical evidence in these types of cases. (For more information, see websites www.FIRSTevidence.org and www.alienhunter.org)

The first official 'alien abduction' occurred on the 19th September 1961. Betty and Barney Hill were driving home in their car. They noticed a large white star trailing their vehicle. At one point Barney felt an urge to stop the car. They both stared at the object, which they described as being shaped like a banana or a pancake. The couple then got back into their car and carried on with their journey home. On their way back they both experienced a beeping noise, which years later, they described as sounding like a microwave oven. The UFO disappeared soon after and the relieved couple eventually arrived home. The first strange thing the couple noticed was that parts of the car's paint had been stripped to reveal metal. Barney also noticed his shoes had been scuffed as if he had been dragged along. The couple could also not account for two hours of their journey. This particular phenomenon has since been popularly termed 'missing time'. Soon after, Betty began experiencing nightmares, featuring beings with cat like eyes intent on kidnapping them both. Eventually on the recommendation of a physician the Hills received hypnotic regression with a view to getting to the root of Betty's trauma. What surfaced was what many in Ufology are familiar with today. The Hills recall being taken on board a craft and receiving a medical examination. Following this, Betty reports being shown a star map, which the beings stated depicted places they had visited. Astronomer Majorie Fish decided to analyse drawings made by Betty of this map. She plotted the location of all stars within a radius of 50 light years of Earth and selected those that had the most likelihood of containing habitable planets. A close match was found with the system of Zeta Reticuli. [3]

Since this case many other alleged abductee accounts have surfaced following hypnotic regressions. Critics point out that these are purely cases of 'false memory syndrome' or confabulation and have no basis in fact. Supporters of the phenomenon argue that the ET hypothesis is backed up by a strong degree of physical evidence such as strange scars, foreign objects or implants, which have shown up on X-rays, some of which have been removed (see photographs opposite). Alleged abductees have been said to be 'missing' by relatives and friends (including cases where both parents cannot find each other) at the time of abduction. There is at least one case involving witnesses to an abduction and multiple witness UFO sightings on the part of the abductees. [4] There have also been a number of cases of young children relaying conscious accounts of medical examinations by other worldly beings. The common theme that abduction researchers espouse from their studies, is that the primary objective during the abduction is the removal of reproductive material; sperm from males and ova from females. Following this abductees often report being shown hybrids - or a cross between the ETs and humans. Speculation following these scenarios lead many researchers to conclude that some kind

Figure 3 **(below):**
A mutilated sheep found on the 3rd May 2002, on a farm near Welshpool, UK. Phil Hoyle (UFO Investigation Unit, Shrewsbury) investigated the cadaver, part of his report is as follows: "...the dead animal that was found that morning was a 6-year-old ewe. It was discovered approximately 250 metres from the farmhouse on the side of a low hill, the other side of the hill was a now disused quarry. The farmer took me to the animal's location, the animal was lying on its back, and it had a 60 mm elongated hole on its left groin and another similar hole on the right groin. The removal of tissue on the head was very extensive particularly on the animals left side lower jaw, it had been cleanly excised and sharp straight cuts were clearly visible. Both eyes were missing, the tongue, the whole of the throat leading down the neck in to the spinal column was stripped bare, the end of the snout was also missing. The extent of the tissue removal looked very similar to the cattle mutilations seen in the U.S, there were no apparent signs of secondary predator attack and both ears were intact and with the ear tag still in place."

of cross breeding programme may be taking place and quite possibly been taking place for thousands of years.

As stated earlier, communication does sometimes take place between the abductors and their victims, however, researchers find that the information imparted from the 'alien being' is often contradictory or reticent. Researchers, looking for historical examples of ET abduction, have drawn parallels with the myths and legends contained in Fairy folklore. For example, in Evans-Wentz's *The Fairy Faith in Celtic Countries* (1911), a number of references are made to short entities, greyish in colour with many accounts using the term 'abduction', which pre-dates its initial use in Ufology in the early 1960s.

ANIMAL MUTILATIONS

Occurring within Ufology is a bizarre phenomenon called Animal Mutilations. Here, animals, normally horses or cattle, are found dead with parts of their anatomy removed, such as their eyes, ears, tongue, reproductive organs and amputation of limbs all in a skillful, intricate manner. Scientists who have analysed these unfortunate victims have concluded they have been cut with a tool emitting great heat, possibly a laser. This fact obviously rules out natural predators. Interestingly, scavengers are known to not even approach these dead carcasses and sometimes the animal doesn't exhibit injury. Other signs can be complete blood loss or a lack of rigor mortis. The process of draining such a large body of fluids, often all the animal's blood, requires a lab setting and highly sophisticated equipment - something certainly not commonly found on cattle ranges and in forests! The process of removing all traces of those fluids from the body and the surrounding environment requires a technology not currently found in the scientific public arena. To add to the perplexity of this phenomenon, the injuries noted on some cadavers indicate they have been dropped from a great height!

UFOs are often seen in the vicinity of these bizarre surgical procedures and one of the earliest recorded Animal Mutilations was that of a

horse named Lady in 1967. A young doctor named John Altschuler, medical haematologist and pathologist came across the dead animal on a ranch in the San Luis Valley of Colorado. He was struck by clean, surgical precision of the cuts and the fact there was absolutely no blood in or around the animal. In an interview with Linda Moulton Howe for

her book, *An Alien Harvest* Dr. Altshuler stated:

"Most amazing was the lack of blood. I have done hundreds of autopsies. You can't cut into a body without getting some blood. But there was no blood on the skin or on the ground. No blood anywhere. Then inside the horse's chest, I remember the lack of organs. Whoever did the cutting took the horse's heart, lungs, and thyroid. The mediastinum was completely empty and dry. How do you get the heart out without blood? It was an incredible dissection of organs without any evidence of blood." [5]

Many accounts stem from the US but animal mutilation is a worldwide phenomenon. In June 2001, for example, 57 sheep and lambs were found dead over the course of five weeks in a field on a farm in the UK. Typical 'skillful' autopsy procedures were noted on the dead animals. Interestingly, the farmer who owned the area once witnessed a large UFO over the very field, coincidence?

Once again Phil Hoyle relates:

"On Saturday mid-morning I called to the farm to ask Dave if I could examine the ground markings in the field where the 24 sheep had disappeared now that the snow had melted. Dave gave me permission but said I would have to go alone, as he was very busy with his farm work. He said that before I left he wanted to show me a dead sheep he had discovered a few days before in a field at the back of the farm.(see figure 4)

The animal was only 60 to 80 feet from the farmhouse on a slight bank, the ani-

mal had been clearly eaten by predators at some point, the sheep was entangled in fence wire and large quantities of wool were spread around the carcass. Dave stated that when he discovered the animal he noticed that its left ear was missing and the cuts to its head looked very precise, the majority of the carcass that had been eaten had taken place after he first discovered the animal.

On examination of the animal the neck and especially the ribcage could clearly be identified as been eaten by predators, the exposure of the face and jaw did look very precise and I think there is a good possibility that the animal was mutilated first and eaten by predators later. The location of the carcass right next to the farmhouse would give anyone cause for concern, a much greater examination of the area must be a top priority if we are not going to miss vital clues to the cause of this phenomena."

CROP CIRCLES

For many summers now in England artwork has been appearing in crops across many fields. Affectionately known as crop circles, these conundrums have become more and more intricate each season. The phenomenon is now worldwide occurring in more than 70 countries. As well as crop, formations are also occurring in ice, treetops and sand. Balls of light have been spotted near and around areas where formations have appeared and most researchers agree that the vast majority are hoaxes. There are however, a remaining 20% that have some interesting and unexplainable characteristics. These include the bending of the crop at the node without snapping and molecular changes in the plant structure, i.e. cell walls becoming swollen or enlarged. In some cases the ground underneath the formation appears dehydrated even after heavy rain and radiation levels in crop circles have been measured up to 10 times above the average. In an article in the *Sunday Times Magazine* dated 15th September 2002, Diane Conrad, a geologist from Utah commented on some soil samples taken from a formation:

"I couldn't understand the results, the soil seems to have been subjected to an intense heat of 500 to 1,500 degrees Celsius and yet the plants were not incinerated. They were not even singed..." [6]

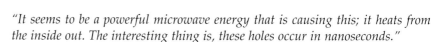

Later in the same article the Michigan biophysicist W E Levengood , mentions a curious anomaly he has researched on plant stems, which are pinhead-sized holes. He comments:

"It seems to be a powerful microwave energy that is causing this; it heats from the inside out. The interesting thing is, these holes occur in nanoseconds."

As well as human hoaxes many other theories have been put forward including the 'plasma vortex theory', whereby plasma vortices form in the sky and strike down into the field creating a formation. As the formations have become more complex, however, this theory has lost ground.

Is there an historical component to crop circles? The earliest recorded formation in England is detailed in a publication from 1686 entitled the *Natural History of Staffordshire* by Professor R Plot. He described 'fairy rings' or formations of circles appearing in fields across the county of Staffordshire, some of them in groups of three or more. His analysis noted circles having a diameter of 40 yards or more, dehydrated soil under the formation and a white sulphurous residue. [7]

Possibly the earliest illustration of a crop formation is that depicted in this woodcut from 1678 (above left). Whether this is a work of fiction or not is open to question but it remains a possible historical reference.

Figure 6) The Moire Pattern (below): One of the more intricate crop circle formations, which was discovered on July 22nd 2000 at Avebury, Trulsoe, UK. You can appreciate its size by looking at the tiny figures standing in the formation.

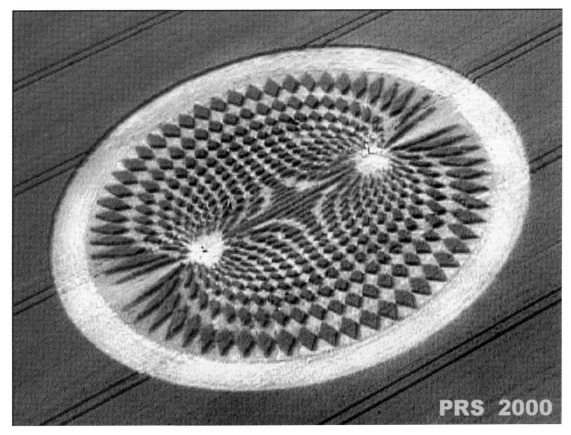

PRS 2000

Astronomer Gerald S Hawkins, former Chairman of the Astronomy Department at Boston University, noticed that some crop formations embodied geometric theorems. For example, one formation featured an equilateral triangle fitting between an outer and inner circle. The outer circle being precisely four times that of the inner circle. He also noted other patterns involved a diatonic ratio, whereby the numerical relationships between the patterns represented a scale of musical notes. Hawkins found the principles of Euclidean geometry in some of the circles, which could be used to prove the four known theorems. He also discovered a

Courtesy of Peter Sorensen © 2000 http://www.cropcircleconnector.com/sorensen

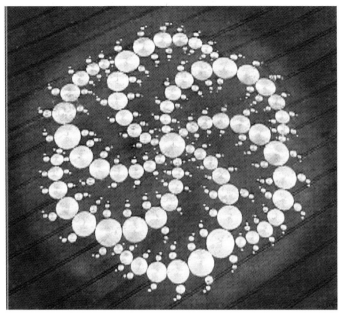

Courtesy of Peter Sorensen © 2001

fifth theorem from which he could derive the other four. Hawkins challenged readers of *Science News* and the *Mathematical Teacher* to come up with the fifth theorem, giving only the four variations. No one was successful. In 1995, however, Hawkins reported: *"...the crop circle makers... showed knowledge of this fifth theorem."* One pattern fitted Hawkins theorem!

Crop circle researcher **Peter Sorenson** has been researching and photographing crop circles for many years. here are two of what he and many others consider to be the most complex formations to date.

THE GALAXY
PRS 2001

Crop circles represent an annual conundrum to researchers worldwide. One cannot rule out a non-human intelligence behind at least some of the formations that grace the countryside each year inspiring curiosity in the minds of thousands of people.

RELIGIOUS REACTION & OFFICIAL ANNOUNCEMENTS

There have been some interesting developments in the Catholic Church regarding their stance on UFOs and extraterrestrials. In 1997 the Pope invited a team of top astronomers to try and locate 'the fingerprints of God' amongst the chaos of the universe. To this end, the Vatican has constructed one of the most powerful observatories on Earth. It is located at Mt Graham in Arizona and consists of two telescopes. One is an optical and the other an infrared system. Both are designed to seek out those star systems, which could give rise to life. Another fact which some may find astonishing is that the Pope sent a personal blessing in the form of a video to the organisers and those attending a UFO conference in December 1999 in Acapulco, Mexico.

Father Corrado Balducci is a renowned exorcist and expert on demonology. Listed in the Vatican directory as a priest of honour since 1964, he is also an official member of the papal household or family and close to the Pope. In 1998 he went on the record stating:

"Extraterrestrials exist and there is no conflict between a belief in aliens and the Christian faith. Their existence can no longer be denied, for there is too much evidence for the existence of extraterrestrials and flying saucers." [9]

In 1999, a 90 page report *Les OVNI et la Defense: A quoi doiton se preparer (UFOs and Defence: What must we be prepared for)*, was written by the Committee for In-Depth Studies (COMETA) at the French Institute of Higher Studies for National Defense (IHEDN). It concluded that the physical reality of UFOs, under the control of intelligent beings, was 'almost certain'. Another part of the report stated: *"...that the extraterrestrial hypothesis is by far the best scientific hypothesis..."* This paper was submitted to the then President Jacques Chirac and Prime Minister Lionel Jospin prior to general release. What made this report fascinating was that COMETA consisted of four Generals, an Admiral and a chief National Police superintendent. The preface was by an Air Force General and an introduction by a former president of the National Centre for Space Studies (CNES) (the French equivalent of NASA.) These were all people with good scientific training in several technical disciplines. Jean Sider, an author, commented on the report:

"It is the first time in France, even in Europe, and maybe in the world, that these unusual manifestations are admitted publicly under the cover of a body close to the Ministry of Defense (IHEDN) as being possibly created by an unknown intelligence, maybe extraterrestrial." [10]

Figure 7) The Galaxy (page 24): This formation made national news and TV across the UK. It consists of 409 perfectly aligned circles (some of which are 70ft in diameter) almost 1000ft across.
It appeared on the morning of Sunday 12th August 2001 at Tan Hill, Alton Barnes in Wiltshire. These formations appear overnight. Could a group of hoaxers create something of this size and complexity in darkness?

In October 2001, the former Chilean Chief of Naval Operations, Admiral Jorge Martinez declared: *"UFOs are real"*. The ex-CNO made the statement during an interview with a Chilean television network. The retired Admiral admitted that he personally witnessed the sighting of two UFOs at sea. Rodrigo Ugarte, the Teletrece interviewer who interviewed Admiral Martinez mentioned to the Miami UFO Center that there were many other officers that described similar events but did not want to go on the air with their accounts.[11]

ASTRONOMY & NASA

There are more stars in the universe than there are grains of sand on all the beaches of the world. The number of stars that astronomers have located in the universe depends on how 'located' is defined. One can take the number of stars in the Milky Way as 'average' and multiply this by the number of known galaxies: $(200 \times 10^9) \times (1 \times 10^9) = 200 \times 10^{18}$.

While working as a radio astronomer at the National Radio Astronomy Observatory in Green Bank, West Virginia, Dr. Frank Drake (now Chairman of the Board of Trustees of the SETI Institute) conceived an approach to bind the terms involved in estimating the number of technological civilisations that may exist in our galaxy. The Drake Equation, as it has come to be known, was first presented by Drake in 1961 and identifies specific factors thought to play a role in the development of such civilisations. Although there is no unique solution to this equation, it is a gen-

$$N = R*FP*NE*F1*FI*FC* L$$

Where:

$N =$ NUMBER OF COMMUNICATING CIVILISATIONS IN A GALAXY
$R =$ RATE OF STAR FORMATION
$Fp =$ FRACTION OF STARS WITH PLANETARY SYSTEMS
$Ne =$ ECOLOGICALLY SUITABLE PLANETS
$F1 =$ FRACTION OF PLANETS ON WHICH LIFE OCCURS
$Fi =$ FRACTION OF PLANETS WITH LIFE AND INTELLIGENT LIFE
$Fc =$ FRACTION WITH COMMUNICATION CAPABILITIES LIKE OURS
$L =$ LIFE TIME OF SUCH A CIVILISATION

erally accepted tool used by the scientific community to examine these factors. Drake's equation calculates the number of communicating civilisations in a galaxy.

Over the last few years many extra solar planets have been discovered, therefore, estimates for many of these variables will have increased greatly. Many astronomers now believe there are parallel or multi-universes thus increasing the chance of extraterrestrial civilisations even further. In order to traverse across the universe, however, any intelligence will have to overcome the great distances involved. There are basically two methods. The first involves exceeding the speed of light, which is 186,000 miles per hour. At the speed of light, however, Einstein's Theory of Relativity states that infinite amounts of mass and energy would be required. This, however, is only the case if the spacecraft is propelled or pushed from outside. It does not apply to an internal power source! The second method is to warp space and time. Here the destination would be pulled towards the spacecraft rather than the spacecraft travelling towards the destination. Some theorists have concluded that a craft would need to be surrounded by 'exotic particles'. By using certain mathematical calculations, Einstein's equations can show that 'Tachyon particles' have a minimum speed of light and a maximum speed of infinity.[12] The craft and its crew would have to be converted into Tachyon particles for this to work! Another concept that is quite popular in Astrophysics is that of Wormholes, which are theoretical funnel shaped holes in the universe. Physicists believe that short cuts created by warping space and time could link two separate parts of the universe and these 'portholes' could provide a gateway to traverse vast distances across space and time almost instantaneously.

SEARCH FOR EXTRATERRESTRIAL INTELLIGENCE (SETI)

The Search for Extraterrestrial Intelligence (SETI) has its origins with mathematician Carl Friedrich Gauss (1777-1855). He had the idea of making contact by cutting a figure into a large area of forest in Central Asia into the shape of the Theorem of Pitagora. Later Charles Cross (1842-1888) proposed the use of a mirror to reflect solar light towards Mars.

In modern times the Search for Extraterrestrial Intelligence (SETI) began in 1960 when a number of scientists got together and postulated the idea that ETs may be sending out radio waves from their planets. In the spring of 1960 *Project Ozma* was set up, consisting of a team of radio astronomers listening out for signals from space. The results of this were disappointing; with billions of stars to scan, it was like looking for a needle in a haystack. In 1992 *Project Cyclops* was dreamt up with an array of radio telescopes to search the heavens. The project was scrapped, as its cost was a prohibitive $6 billion! In 1992 NASA committed $58m to a project to scan thousands of stars for life utilising the 305m radio telescope at Arecibo, Puerto Rico. This project was also scrapped after one year.

The spirit of SETI lives on in a number of projects including the Allen Telescope Array, named after the co-founder of Microsoft, Paul Allen. It consists of a radio telescope formed by 700 parabolas 4 metres each. Another SETI initiative is *Project Phoenix*, currently halfway through its programme; it is scanning 1000 nearby sunlike stars utilising the world's largest radio telescopes.

Another branch of SETI, Optical SETI, is concerned with the optical rather than the radio wave spectrum. Its aim is to search for signs of life by utilising sensitive instruments that can detect photons of light emitted from distant star systems. A group has been set up at the University of

Berkeley and Santa Cruz in California. And they plan to construct three light detectors (photo multipliers) that will search for bright pulses of light that arrive in a short space of time (less than one billionth of a second). Another similar project is planned at Princeton and Harvard and another at the University of Columbus, Ohio. Only time will tell how fruitful these projects prove.

SOURCES

1) Ex-pilot George Filer produces a regular online UFO newsletter at *www.filersfiles-ufo.com*. The Russian report stems from his 4th March 2000 newsletter.

2) Genesis III produced two excellent video documentaries detailing the activity over the skies of Mexico since 1991: *Masters of the Stars* 1994 and *Voyagers of the Sixth Sun* 1996. Genesis III, Box 25962, Munds Park, Az. 86017.

3) Betty and Barney Hills experiences were the basis for John G Fuller's best selling 1966 book *The Interrupted Journey*. Now published under the Dell Pub. Co. It was later turned into a film called *The UFO Incident*.

4) Budd Hopkins is one of the foremost Alien Abduction researchers, having investigated over 700 cases. His three books, *Missing Time* (1981), *Intruders* (1987) and *Witnessed* (1996), are widely regarded by researchers and skeptics alike as comprising the most influential series of books yet published on the abduction phenomenon. He now heads the Intruders Foundation, a non-profit, scientific research and support organisation.

5) *An Alien Harvest - Further Evidence Linking Animal Mutilations and Human Abductions to Alien Life Forms*, by Linda Moulton Howe 1993. Linda is a producer, director, writer of films, videos and scripts, including *A Strange Harvest*, a documentary on the 'cattle mutilation' phenomenon. She has been researching animal mutilations for many years and has established herself as a major authority on this subject. *www.earthfiles.com*

6) Other anomalies in soil samples have been noted too, including the presence of tiny 10-40 micron diameter spheres of unusually pure iron. Sometimes clusters of these very small, perfectly spherical, magnetic particles are found; sometimes larger spheres (40-50 microns in diameter), which are strongly magnetic, are discovered adhering to bits of soil covered, or inter-mixed, with a partially melted glaze of the same material. Diane Conrad is one of a number of scientific consultants working for the BLT Research Team, a non-profit, tax-exempt status research body based in the US, dedicated to researching crop circles. *www.bltresearch.com*

7) *The Natural History of Stafford-shire*. Robert Plott (spelled "Plot" on title page.) Oxford, 1686. (Pages 7-21 describe what may be 17th-Century fairy rings or crop circles.)

8) *The Mowing Devil* woodcut, believed to be the earliest recorded crop circle. Some have speculated that the circles are even older - that Neolithic man was witness to them and, believing them to be the work of the Earth Goddess he worshipped, was inspired to build the great temples of Stonehenge, Avebury, Stanton Drew, Woodhenge and Silbury Hill.

9) *UFO Magazine*, Nov/Dec 2001 pages 10-11. Published by Quest Publications International Ltd, Valley Farm Way, Wakefield Road, Stourton, Leeds LS10 1SE

Balducci was interviewed on the Italian TV programme *Mysterious Italy* on 24th November 1986. Amongst his comments was the following quote:

"It is probable that there are other beings, that is not very strange, because among the human and angelic nature, of which we have the theological certainty, there is a discrepancy. And among this man, in whom the spirit is subordinate as to the matter, and the Angels that are alone spirit, are probable that they exist of the beings that have spirit with the very less matter and body of that, that we have. They could be those that we call UFO, these persons that would appear with these wagons."

10) Good, Timothy: *Unearthly Disclosure*, Published by Century 2000.
pp1-3. COMETA, *Les OVNI et la Defense: A quoi-on se preparer*, GS Presse Communication, 79-83 rue Baudin, 92309 Levallois-Perret Cedex, France, July 1999.

11) From an article translated by Mario Andrade and published by the Miami UFO Center. 21st October 2001. *http://ufomiami.dventures.com/eng/*
Miami UFO Center, P.O.Box 960771, Miami, Fl. 33296 U.S.A.

12) Tachyons were first proposed by physicist Arnold Sommerfeld, and named by Gerald Feinberg. The word tachyon derives from the Greek (tachus), meaning 'speedy'. Tachyons have the strange properties that, when they lose energy, they gain speed. Consequently, when tachyons gain energy, they slow down. The slowest speed possible for tachyons is the speed of light.

THE ART OF INTERPRETING HISTORICAL EVENTS *Chapter Two*

W hen we analyse accounts of historical UFO sightings and unusual artworks, one needs to ask oneself a series of questions to arrive at an accurate explanation for what the author was trying to communicate. We are left with two possible models depicted below: Model A - a real event or Model B - an imagined event.

MODEL A

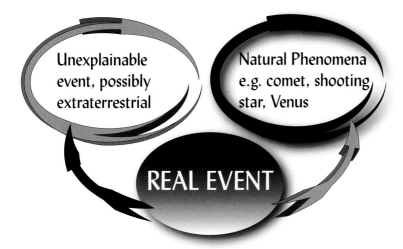

In **Model A**, above, we have a representation of a real event. The author or artist has communicated a real event. We are now left with two explanations, either an unexplainable event - possibly extraterrestrial, is being described, or, a natural phenomenon. About 95% of UFO sightings turn out to be natural phenomenon, with the remaining 5% being unexplainable in natural terms. Some of these could be extraterrestrial in origin. Natural phenomenon can be a variety of objects including: aircraft, meteors, comets, stars (notably Venus), birds and piezoelectric phenomena - created by tectonic action on quartz in the ground producing luminous lights in the sky and hallucinations.

The photograph on the opposite page is of a set of hieroglyphs from a temple in Abydos, Egypt.(see page 35)

Figure 1) A section from the Bayeux Tapestry.
In this example (right), what possibly appears to be a sighting of a UFO has a purely natural explanation. It is in fact the sighting of Halley's Comet in 1066, as depicted in the Bayeux Tapestry.
© Reading Museum

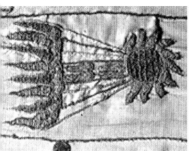

Figure 2) The Oldest UFO Photograph?
This photograph (right) is sometimes touted in Ufology as the world's oldest UFO photo. It was taken in Drobak, Norway in July 1909. What appears to be a large UFO hovering off shore is in fact a lenticular cloud.

© Science & Vie Issue 345, 1946

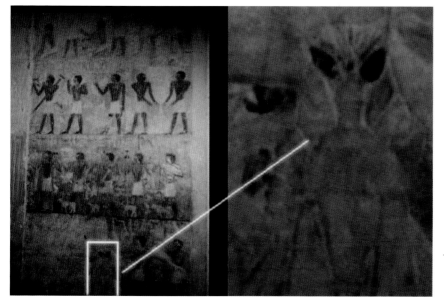

Figure 3 (top left): This is a popular image and has done the rounds on many web-sites of the unexplained. It is often referred to as **'The Abydos temple helicopter'**. It is a set of hieroglyphs from a temple in Abydos, Egypt. On examination it looks like one can see a helicopter, an aircraft and possibly a tank! The solution to this bizarre artifact is that it is a palimpsest, which is defined as a manu-script, typically of papyrus or parchment that has been written on more than once. With the earlier writing incompletely erased and often legible over time, some of the plaster on the wall that once cov-ered Seti's titulary has fallen away, leaving some superimposed signs looking like mod-ern day technology.

© Bonechi

Figures 4 & 5 (above & left): This painting appears to show a bipedal **insectiod entity** on an Egyptian wall in the tomb of Ptah-Hotep, North Saqqara. Not all is as it seems though. It is in fact a vase with food offerings. Shown on the left is another version of the same image from Bonechi's All of Egypt, an easy to obtain Egyptian guide. Thanks to Cesar Guarde for this information.

MODEL B

In **Model B** (above), the artist/author has communicated an imagined, 'unreal' event. It has no basis in fact. This scenario has a number of explanations: firstly, the artist could be communicating a fictional story, possibly one handed down over generations. In the case of artwork it could be a painting featuring religious allegory. Model B would of course include hoax cases!

Various psychologists have cast their minds at the UFO phenomenon. In particular, Swiss psychologist Carl Gustav Jung put forward his views in his 1957 book *Flying Saucers: A myth of modern things seen in the sky.* Jung formed the idea that the UFO phenomenon is not real and UFOs can be viewed as the recurrence of an ancient archetype dressed in modern clothing. For Jung, it was characteristic of modern times that the archetype takes the form of an object or a 'technical construction' in order to avoid the 'odiousness of mythological personification', because everything that looks technical goes down without much difficulty with mod-

Figure 6 (left):
An example of a
hoax, This photograph
was most probably cre-
ated with computer
editing software.
Two humanoid figures
and a rocket appear on
the walls of this temple
in Kush (Nubia),
Egypt.

ern man. The problem with Jung's exotic theory, as this book demonstrates, is that this modern technological 'archetype' has been around for a very long time and therefore cannot be considered a modern archetype expressing itself in the minds of people.

Occasionally, the discovery of new elements in art has caused the rewriting of history. Could the depiction of UFOs in historical artwork and literature initiate another revision? Art like science and religion fulfils our innate urge to comprehend ourselves and the universe and can penetrate to the core of our being. Artists articulate shared beliefs and values and express them to their audience. Inspiration in itself is an interesting concept. Some people believe that artists can be inspired by a higher power that acts through the artist. Possibly we witness this in some of the religious artwork. If we consider for one moment that extraterrestrials have been visiting our planet for thousands of years, we cannot rule out the idea that they may have inspired people in many differing fields of human culture including the Arts.

Ever since prehistory, man has gazed up at the heavens and expressed celestial happenings in the form of art. This book provides a chronicle of these celestial representations. Evidence of this is shown early on in the chapter on prehistoric art, with flying saucers depicted on the walls of Palaeolithic caves in Southern France. Talking openly about unusual phenomena, like UFOs, would have been perilous in times like the Inquisition. Therefore the subtle insertion of a UFO in a painting would have been a method for overcoming the censorship in those bleak periods. An example of this is shown on the next page.

Figure 7)
A detail from 'The
Madonna and Saint
Giovannino '(right):
School of Lippi 1406 –
1469 (see page 84)
Chapter Five, on
Western Religious
Artwork and UFOs.
© Coutesy of the Palazzo
Vecchio, Italy

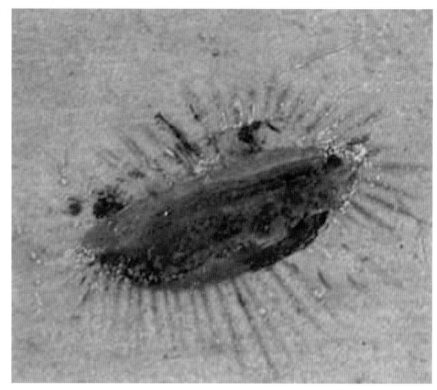

Is this really a cloud? Art historians would have us believe that it is just one of many symbols that accompany the Madonna in numerous Renaissance paintings. To many, however, it looks suspiciously like a flying saucer emanating light or an energy field.

Just as art has its movements, so vocabulary expands and changes over generations as new ideas and concepts come into society's vernacular. In terms of a genuine extraterrestrial encounter, one has to ask oneself what adjectives the historical author would have used. The term 'extraterrestrial' would not have existed hundreds of years ago, therefore if an ancient writer described a sighting of an ET craft he was likely to use metaphors like 'silver shield', 'chariot' or 'dragon'. These are exactly the kind of terms that will crop up in the section on creation stories from ancient civilisations around the globe. The observer of the phenomenon tried to clothe his/her experience in the best terms of the day. Through artistic images and writings from the past and present, one receives an insight into phenomena that occupied the minds of ancient people. One can only wonder at what people thought in the 16th Century on reading accounts of airborne objects, and strange aerial depictions in paintings.

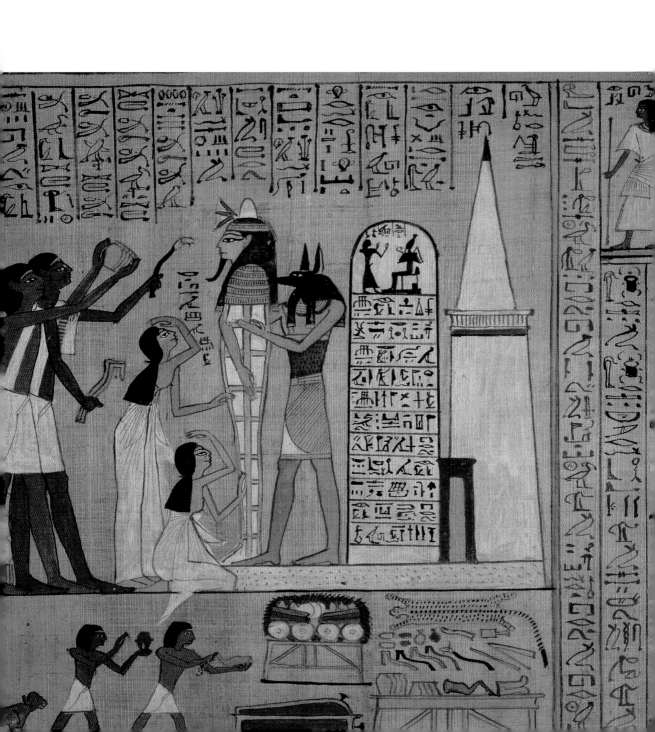

CREATION STORIES *Chapter Three*

This chapter attempts to bring together the various creation myths and legends of cultures all across the globe. Common threads will appear and it will become apparent that the one characteristic these stories have is that of beings from elsewhere, appearing with 'Godlike' powers and trying to uplift and develop that particular culture. Are these accounts simply works of fiction handed down over generations or is there some kernel of truth? We will be looking for clues in many of the world's continents: North and South America, Asia, Europe, Africa and Australasia.

1) ASIA
India & the Orient

The Indian *Vedas* provide a rich source of possible UFO material. They consist of three main texts, the *Bhagavata Purana* (900 AD), the *Mahabharata* and the *Ramayana* (600-500 BC). The actual content of these texts is considered to be much older and according to native Indian tradition they date back to at least 3000 BC. In 1931 James Churchwood brought to the attention of the western world the many descriptions of flying vehicles in these historical texts. The term for these flying vehicles is Vimanas.

"In the Vedic literature of India, there are many descriptions of flying machines that are generally called vimanas. These fall into two categories: (1) manmade craft that resemble airplanes and fly with the aid of birdlike wings, and (2) unstreamlined structures that fly in a mysterious manner and are generally not made by human beings. The machines in category (1) are described mainly in medieval, secular Sanskrit works dealing with architecture, automata, military siege engines, and other mechanical contrivances. Those in category (2) are described in ancient works such as the Rig Veda, the Mahabharata, the Ramayana, and the Puranas, and they have many features reminiscent of UFOs."

"There are ancient Indian accounts of manmade wooden vehicles that flew with wings in the manner of modern airplanes. Although these wooden vehicles were also called vimanas, most vimanas were not at all like airplanes. The more typical vimanas had flight characteristics resembling those reported for UFOs, and the beings associated with them were said to possess powers similar to those presently ascribed to UFO entities. An interesting example of a vimana is the fly-

The image on the opposite page is the Papyrus of Hunefer from the Book of the Dead (1310BC)

© The British Museum Courtesy of the Trustees of The British Museum

ing machine which Salva, an ancient Indian king, acquired from Maya Danava, an inhabitant of a planetary system called Taltala." [1]

The ancient Indian epic *Ramayana* describes a Vimana as a double deck, circular aircraft with portholes and a dome. It flew with the *'speed of the wind'* and gave forth a *'melodious sound'*. There were at least four different types of Vimanas; some saucer shaped, some blimp like, some triangular and others like long cylinders (cigar shaped airships). The ancient Indian texts on Vimanas are so numerous it would take volumes to relate what they had to say.

In the Sanskrit *Samarangana Sutradhara*, we have a description of a Vimana:

"Strong and durable must the body of the Vimana be made, like a great flying bird of light material. Inside one must put the mercury engine with its iron heating apparatus underneath. By means of the power latent in the mercury which sets the driving whirlwind in motion, a man sitting inside may travel a great distance in the sky. The movements of the Vimana are such that it can vertically ascend, vertically descend, and move slanting forwards and backwards. With the help of the machines human beings can fly in the air and heavenly beings can come down to earth."

"One time while King Citaketu was travelling in outer space on a brilliantly effulgent airplane given to him by Lord Vishnu, he saw Lord Siva..."The arrows released by Lord Siva appeared like fiery beams emanating from the sun globe and covered the three residential airplanes, which could then no longer be seen." [2]

In the *Mahabharata*, an ancient Indian poem of enormous length, we learn that an individual named Asura Maya had a Vimana measuring twelve cubits in circumference, with four strong wheels.
These ancient texts are filled with references to Gods who fought battles in the sky using Vimanas equipped with weapons as deadly as any we can deploy in these more enlightened times. For example, in the *Mahabharata's Drona Parva*, we find two types of weapons described: the Agnaya Weapon, an eyewitness account of the Agnaya reads like a nuclear weapon and the Brahma Weapon (or Indra's dart) which appears to work on a vibrationary principle.

Figure 3) Eduard Meier took this photo on the 3rd July 1964 (right): A disc shaped UFO was seen flying around the Ashoka Ashram, Mehrauli, India. Many people witnessed this event as Meier took this photo. The leader of the Ashram, V.B. Dharmawara, has gone on record stating he had witnessed UFOs around the Ashram. This particular Ashram is named after King Ashoka who ruled the Mauryan Empire in Northern India (C.268-239 BC). He later became a Buddhist and helped extend the Buddhist tradition in India. It is said that the Indian Emperor Ashoka, was aware of advanced vehicles and other 'futuristic weapons' that had destroyed the ancient Indian 'Rama Empire' several thousand years before.

© *Eduard Meier*

Rogue adventurer and maverick archaeologist David Hatcher Childress, makes some intriguing comments on King Ashoka in his book *The Anti-Gravity Handbook*:

"The Indian Emperor Ashoka started a 'Secret Society of the Nine Unknown Men': great Indian scientists who were supposed to catalogue the many sciences. Ashoka kept their work secret because he was afraid that the advanced science catalogued by these men, culled from ancient Indian sources, would be used for the evil purpose of war, which Ashoka was strongly against, having been converted to Buddhism after defeating a rival army in a bloody battle. The Nine Unknown Men wrote a total of nine books, presumably one each. Book number one was 'The Secrets of Gravitation!' This book, known to historians, but not actually seen by

them dealt chiefly with 'gravity control'. It is presumably still around somewhere, kept in a secret library in India, Tibet or elsewhere (perhaps even in North America somewhere). One can certainly understand Ashoka's reasoning for wanting to keep such knowledge a secret, assuming it exists. Ashoka was also aware of devastating wars using such advanced vehicles and other 'futuristic weapons' that had destroyed the ancient Indian Rama Empire several thousand years before.

Only a few years ago, the Chinese discovered some Sanskrit documents in Lhasa, Tibet and sent them to the University of Chandrigarh to be translated. Dr. Ruth Reyna of the University said recently that the documents contain directions for building interstellar spaceships! Their method of propulsion, she said, was 'anti-gravitational' and was based upon a system analogous to that of 'laghima', the unknown power of the ego existing in man's physiological makeup, 'a centrifugal force strong enough to counteract all gravitational pull'. According to Hindu Yogis, it is this 'laghima' which enables a person to levitate. Dr. Reyna said that on board these machines, which were called 'Astras' by the text, the ancient Indians could have sent a detachment of men onto any planet, according to the document, which is thought to be thousands of years old. The manuscripts were also said to reveal the secret of 'antima'; 'the cap of invisibility' and 'garima'; 'how to become as heavy as a mountain of lead'. Naturally, Indian scientists did not take the texts very seriously, but then became more positive about the value of them when the Chinese announced that they were including certain parts of the data for study in their space program! This was one of the first instances of a government admitting to be researching anti-gravity. The manuscripts did not say definitely that interplanetary travel was ever made but did mention, of all things, a planned trip to the Moon, though it is not clear whether this trip was actually carried out.

"When the Rishi City of Mohenjodaro was excavated by archaeologists in the last century, they found skeletons just lying in the streets, some of them holding hands, as if some great doom had suddenly overtaken them. These skeletons are among the most radioactive ever found, on a par with those found at Hiroshima and Nagasaki. Ancient cities whose brick and stonewalls have literally been vitrified, that is-fused together, can be found in India, Ireland, Scotland, France, Turkey and other places. There is no logical explanation for the vitrification of stone forts and cities, except from an atomic blast. Furthermore, at Mohenjo-Daro, a well planned city laid on a grid, with a plumbing system superior to those used in Pakistan and India today, the streets were littered with 'black lumps of glass'. These globs of glass were discovered to be clay pots that had melted under intense heat!" [3]

According to the Sanskrit scholar V.R. Ramachandran Dikshitar, the Oxford Professor who wrote *War in Ancient India* in 1944:

" No question can be more interesting in the present circumstances of the world than India's contribution to the science of aeronautics. There are numerous illustrations in our vast Puranic and epic literature to show how well and wonder-

fully the ancient Indians conquered the air. To glibly characterise everything found in this literature as imaginary and summarily dismiss it as unreal has been the practice of both Western and Eastern scholars until very recently. The very idea indeed was ridiculed and people went so far as to assert that it was physically impossible for man to use flying machines. But today what with balloons, aeroplanes and other flying machines, a great change has come over our ideas on the subject."

Says Dr. Dikshitar:

"...the flying vimana of Rama or Ravana was set down as but a dream of the mythographer till aeroplanes and zeppelins of the present century saw the light of day. The mohanastra or the 'arrow of unconsciousness' of old was until very recently a creature of legend till we heard the other day of bombs discharging poisonous gases. We owe much to the energetic scientists and researchers who plod persistently and carry their torches deep down into the caves and excavations of old and dig out valid testimonials pointing to the misty antiquity of the wonderful creations of humanity."

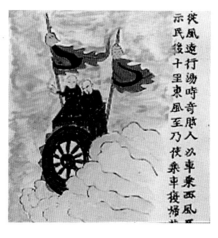

Dikshitar also mentions that in Vedic literature, in one of the *Brahmanas*, the concept of a ship that sails heavenwards:

"The ship is the Agniliotra of which the Ahavaniya and Garhapatya fires represent the two sides bound heavenward, and the steersman is the Agnihotrin who offers milk to the three Agnis. Again, in the still earlier Rg Veda Samhita we read that the Asvins conveyed the rescued Bhujya safely by means of winged ships. The latter may refer to the aerial navigation in the earliest times."

Commenting on the famous vimana text the *Vaimanika Shastra*, he says:

" In the recently published Samarangana Sutradhara of Bhoja, a whole chapter of about 230 stanzas is devoted to the principles of construction underlying the various flying machines and other engines used for military and other purposes. The various advantages of using machines, especially flying ones, are given elaborately. Special mention is made for their attacking visible as well as invisible objects, of their use at one's will and pleasure, of their uninterrupted movements, of their strength and durability, in short of their capability to do in the air all that is done on earth. After enumerating and explaining a number of other advantages, the author concludes that even impossible things could be affected through them. Three movements are usually ascribed to these machines, ascending, cruising, thousands of miles in the atmosphere and lastly descending. It is said that in an aerial car one can mount to the Surya-mandala, travel throughout the regions of air above the sea and the earth. These cars are said to move so fast as to make a noise that could be heard faintly from the ground. Still some writers have expressed a doubt and asked "Was that true?" But the evidence in its favor is overwhelming."

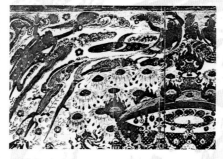

Figure 5 (left):
This is a wall painting from the Mogao cave in the Kansu province dated to the Tang Dynasty 713-762 BC. You can see a number of saucer shaped objects in the picture.
© China Im Aufbau No: 6 Nov/dec 1978

As well as descriptions of flying vehicles these ancient texts even describe other planetary worlds. The *Puranas* speak of 400,000 humanlike races living on various planets. The Vedic humanoids are varied in appearance, some of them like the Gandharvas and Siddhas are said to have beautiful human forms. In contrast others are said to be ugly and frightening. Many of these beings are described as having special powers of siddhis. Some are described as being more developed than others.

The Vedic worldview is that all living beings are souls existing in a physical body. The soul is endowed with consciousness and transmi-

Figure 6 (left):
An artistic reproduction of a relief found in a labyrinth in the spurs of the Hunan mountains, on the south shore of Lake Tung Ting, west of Yoyang. Tschi Pen Lao, Professor of Archeology at the University of Peking, discovered this labyrinth. The passage walls were smooth and glazed. The walls of one passage were covered with paintings. They represented animals fleeing in one direction, driven by men on flying shields aiming weapon-like implements at the animals.

Courtesy of Erich Von Däniken
© www.daniken.com

grates from one gross body to another under universal laws. There is a natural process of evolution where more advanced souls attain higher and higher types of bodies. All manifestations emanate from the Supreme Being and individual souls are understood to be parts of the Supreme Being. According to Vedic philosophy, spiritual advancement is the main goal of human life. The various humanoid races are described as having varying outlooks, some are self-centred, some hostile, and others have a more spiritual outlook. Earthlings are described as being descended from several lines at different times and have quite a complex celestial ancestry.

'Bon' - a pre Buddhist Tibetan religion, mentions how a mighty 'friend of virtue and kindness' had appeared on Earth:

"... Egg, created by magical forces of Gods Sa and Bal, exited under the action of its weight from the divine bosom of empty sky. The shell became a defensive armour. The casing defended like armour, and that which is White became a source of strength for heroes. The inner casing became a stronghold for those who dwelt in it... From the very centre of the Egg came a human being, Possessor of magic Force..."

Figure 7(above):
A 100 year old Chinese
illustration depicting a
flying saucer!
Source: UFO Magazine
July 2002

What can we read into this passage? It appears to describe an egg shaped object coming down from above and from within came a being with special powers.

According to the *Gyelrap*, the genealogy of Tibetan kings, originally there were twenty-seven legendary kings. It says of these: *"seven heavenly kings climbed down the ladder of heaven."* The Tibetans called them 'Gods of Light' and once their mission on Earth was complete they returned from whence they came. Intriguingly the oldest Buddhist scriptures are supposed to have fallen to Earth in a little chest.

The sacred Tibetan books are called the *Kantyua* and the *Tantyua*. The *Kantyua* consists of 108 folio volumes, 9 sections and 1083 books. The *Tantyua* consists of 225 volumes and is a commentary on the *Kantyua*. Only about one hundreth of their contents has been translated. Their date of origin is unknown. The *Kantyua* tells of flying 'pearls in the sky' and transparent spheres containing gods who came to visit men.

The 'Dakas' of Mahayana Buddhism were 'sky-travelling beings' and Padmasambhava, the founder of Tibetan Buddhism, is described as having come from heaven carrying writings in an

Figures 8 & 9
(above and right):
These images are from
the 10th Century
Tibetan translation of
the Sanskrit text
Prajnaparamita Sutra,
held at a Japanese
museum. Notice the
two hat shaped objects.
Could these be histori-
cal depictions of UFOs?

Source: Viaggiator del
tempo,
by Peter Kolosimo

unknown language. After teaching a number of people on Earth, he chose one of his pupils to translate his written works. This pupil, Pagur Vaircana describes the departure of Padmasambhava :

"then a cloud and a rainbow appeared in the sky, and the cloud came very close. In the midst of the cloud stood a horse of gold and silver... Everybody could see how it went to meet them (the gods) through the air. When the horse had flown up one ell into the sky, Padmasambhava turned around. Looking for me will be

an endless task, he said and flew away. The king and his retinue were like fish on the sand... when they gazed up, they saw Padmasambhava the size of a raven; when they looked up again they saw him the size of a thrush, and then he was like a fly; the next time he seemed vague and shimmery, the size of a louse's egg. And when they looked up again, they could no longer see him at all." [4]

Researcher Jim Marrs states in his book *Alien Agenda* that:

"In Tibet I have seen records of strange craft in the skies. The Chariots of the Gods most people call them."

Ancient Chinese records mention 'Sons of Heaven'. Haven't we heard similar phrases before in other religions? Huang-Ti is considered to be the most notable. According to Chinese mythology he first appeared in the Huang He River basin. Here he helped the natives in a variety of fields including the sciences. According to Tao sources, after one hundred years of rule he returned to his home star: *"ascended the heavens and became the ruler of the Great Infinite, again turning into the star Syuan Yuan."* Modern astronomers have identified this constellation as the Leo constellation. In the biography of Huang-Ti it is mentioned that he possessed a Changhuan, or dragon and it could cover myriads of miles in a day, and that a human who 'rides' it can reach an age of two thousand years. This seems to indicate an effect on the ageing process and travelling at high velocities. These concepts seem somewhat out of place in ancient Oriental text! [5]

Yves Naud, in his book *UFOs and Extraterrestrials in History* recounts an ancient Chinese story of Hou Yih, an engineer for the Emperor Yao, who decided, 4,300 years ago, to go to the moon with a 'celestial bird.' In the course of the flight, the bird indicated to the traveller the exact movements of the rising, the apogee, and the setting of the sun. Hou Yih thereafter explained that he *"sailed up the current of luminous air."* Could this current have been the exhaust of a rocket?
"He no longer perceived the rotary movement of the sun", the narrator points out. Effectively, contemporary astronauts have noted that, in space, it was not possible to discern the diurnal passage of the sun. And what did the Chinese engineer observe on the moon? He saw *"an horizon which appeared frozen."* To protect himself from the glacial air, he built the 'Palace of the Great Cold.' His wife, Chang Ngo, left to join him on the satellite, which she described as *"a luminous sphere, brilliant as glass, of an enormous size, and very cold."*

THE MESOPOTAMIAN CIVILISATIONS

Researcher Zechariah Sitchin has spent many years deciphering the clay tablets left behind by the Mesopotamian (modern Iraq) civilisations. The first civilisation there was the Sumerians who existed between 5000 BC and flourished as a major civilisation by 3500 BC. The first written form of

language, Cuneiform, was developed here. The Babylonians succeeded them in 1900 BC. In 1976 Sitchin published his account of a 4,000-year-old sacred Babylonian text known as *Enuma Elish*. He claims it is an account of the formation of the solar system 4.6 billion years ago. This text mentions a planet known as Marduk or Nibiru. It is described as a wandering planet, which entered our solar system and collided with a watery planet called Tiamat. The records state following the collision, Tiamat was split into two. One part became Earth shunted by one of Marduk's moons into a new orbit. Marduk came around again and this time collided with the remaining half creating the asteroid belt between Mars and Jupiter. Sitchin maintains the Sumerians called their Gods An-unnn.ki meaning 'those from Heaven to Earth came'. In original Hebrew the term 'heaven' was originally written as two words 'sham' and 'ma'im', literally meaning, 'where the waters were'. This could well be a reference to Tiamat. Thus it could well be that the Gods came from the orbit of Tiamat - Nibiru. Many researchers feel the Gods used Nibiru as a vehicle to traverse through space. Why did the Gods come to Earth? According to Sitchin's interpretation of the texts they came to exploit the Earth's mineral wealth. To aid this process the senior gods created primitive hybrid beings. The Hebrew term 'Nefilim' closely parallels the meaning of the Sumerian term An-unnn.ki, meaning 'those who descended'.

We read the term Nefilim in the Bible:

"When men began to increase in number on the Earth and daughters were born to them, the sons of God saw that the daughters of men were beautiful, and they married any of them they chose... The Nefilim were on the Earth in those days- and also afterwards - when the sons of God went to the daughters of men and had

children by them. They were the heroes of old, men of renown."
(*Genesis 6:1-4*)

To many, the above passage talks of beings coming down to Earth and mating with the female inhabitants. It is often pointed out that the chances of ETs resembling us are extremely remote, but maybe we resemble them? Researcher Alan Alford in his book *Gods of the New Millennium* noted that around 200,000 years ago Homo sapiens suddenly appeared with a 50 per cent increase in brain size, together with language capability and modern anatomy. Alford feels that according to the theory of natural selection, this is statistically near impossible. Could ETs have been responsible for this accelerated development?

Only a tiny percentage of these tablets survive but they leave behind rich imagery of heavenly beings. The following descriptions are taken from a history of Mesopotamia written in the Third Century BC by Berossus, a Babylonian priest whose work survives only in fragments recorded by later Greek historians:

"In the first year there appeared, from that part of the Erythraean sea, which borders upon Babylonia, an animal destitute of reason, by name Oannes, whose whole body (according to the account of Apollodorus) was that of a fish. That under the fish's head he had another head, with feet also below, similar to those of a man, subjoined to the fish's tail. His voice too, and language, was articulated and human, and a representation of him is preserved even to this day." (see figure 10)

Following the Babylonians came the Chaldeans. Greek chronicler Apollodorus from Athens mentioned during the era of King Ammenon the Chaldean, *"appeared the Musarus Oannes, the Annedotus, from the Persian Gulf,"* and later *"a fourth Annedotus, having...the shape of a fish blended with that of a man."* Annedotus translates as 'the repulsive one'. If this were purely a story, would an ancient chronicler describe his God as repulsive? Surely the Gods would have been glorified as pleasing to the eye? Or

Figure 12 (belowleft):
Assyrian relief from the 9th Century BC from Nineveh, now in the British Museum. The Assyrian god Shamash is depicted in his heavenly ship.
© *The British Museum: Courtesy of the Trustees of the British Museum*

maybe the sight of a half-amphibious, half-human God (ET), for our ancestors, was repulsive? [6]

BIBLE STORIES

There are a number of passages in the Bible that can be interpreted as possible references to ETs and UFOs. Probably the most well known biblical reference to a possible UFO is Ezekiel's vision. Ezekiel was a priest deported to Babylon in 597 BC. Five years later he had a series of visions, which lasted for a period of nineteen years. One of them is as follows.

"I looked, and I saw a windstorm coming out of the North - an immense cloud with flashing lightning and surrounded by brilliant light. The centre of the fire looked like glowing metal, and in the fire was what looked like four living creatures. In appearance their form was that of a man, but each of them had four faces and four wings. Their legs were straight, their feet were like those of a calf and gleamed like burnished bronze. Under the wings on their four sides they had the hands of a man. All four of them had faces and wings, and their wings touched one another. Each one went straight ahead, they did not turn as they moved. As I looked at the living creatures, I saw a wheel on the ground beside each creature with its four faces. This was the appearance and structure of the wheels: they sparkled like chrysolite and all four looked alike. Each appeared to be made like a wheel intersecting a wheel. As they moved, they would go in any one of the four directions the creatures faced; the wheels did not turn about as the creatures went. Their rims were high and awesome, and all four rims were full of eyes all round. When the living creatures moved, the wheels beside them moved; and when the living creatures rose from the ground, the wheels also rose. Wherever the spirit would go, they would go, and the wheels would rise along with them, because the spirit of the living creatures was in the wheels."
(*Ezekiel 1:1-28*)

Ezekiel appears to be describing a brightly coloured metallic 'wheel shaped' aerial object. NASA engineer Josef Blumrich became fascinated with Ezekiel's vision and after exhaustive study published a book entitled *The Spaceships of Ezekiel*. He concluded that Ezekiel was describing the landing process of a flying object:

"Ezekiel begins with the fire and the clouds of the braking phase; then he describes the helicopters during the aerodynamic flight; and the radiator of the reactor and the control rockets as the spaceship is hovering; then he observes the functioning of the wheels and the rolling on the ground. Thus, the wheels appear in the text as the very place they become necessary from a functional point of view. This sequence is an additional confirmation that the wheels are retractable and further proof of the accuracy of the description."

A year later the Lord appeared to Ezekiel again. This next piece of text sounds remarkably like a trip in a aerial craft of some kind :

"Then, I beheld ! and lo', a likeness as the appearance of fire; from the appearance of his loins even downwards fire; and from his loins even upwards as the colour of amber. And he put fourth the form of a hand, and took me up by a lock of mine head; and the spirit lifted me up between Earth and the heavens, and brought me in the visions of God to Jerusalem, to the door of the inner gate that looketh toward the north."
(*Ezekiel 8:2-3*)

In 1968 Presbyterian Pastor Barry H Downing PhD published a book entitled *The Bible and Flying Saucers*. This seminal work looked at the *Old* and *New Testaments* for possible UFOs. Starting with the *Old Testament*,

Downing found a number of key biblical events, for example, the 'pillar of cloud' that led Moses and the Israelites out of Egypt and onto the Red Sea and Mt Sinai:

"And the Lord went before them by day in a pillar of a cloud, to lead them in a way; and by night in a pillar of fire, to give them light; to go by day and night: He took not away the pillar of the cloud by day, nor the pillar of fire by night, from before the people."
(*Exodus 13:21-22*)

Once Moses and his group arrived at the Red Sea, again we find the Pillar of Cloud :

"And the Angel of God, which went before the camp of Israel, removed and went-

behind them; and the pillar of cloud went from before their face, and stood between them." (*Exodus 14:19*)
Following this the Red Sea parted

Figure 13:
This series of six photos (left) were taken by an Army Private stationed at Fort Belvoir, Va. in 1957. The photographer and about five or six others witnessed a ring flying overhead, which was estimated to be 60ft in diameter. The Private grabbed his Brownie camera and started taking this series of six photos.
The object started to cover itself in a strange mist. Within 60 seconds the whole object was completely enveloped in a small compact cloud.

© *The Ring Shaped UFO by Ralph Rankow, Flying Saucers UFO Reports Magazine No.4 1967*

and allowed Moses and the Israelites to cross on towards Mt Sinai. Could this cloud have been a UFO, which used its advanced technology to part the sea?

"And the Lord said unto Moses, Lo, I come unto thee in a thick cloud, that the people may hear when I speak with thee, and believe thee forever. And Moses, told the words of the people unto the Lord."
(*Exodus 20:9*)

From reading the above quotes, it seems a UFO is not out of the question. Are there any modern accounts of UFOs and clouds? Consider the following case and associated photographs on the previous page. Perhaps this event, fortunately captured on camera, provides us with a modern insight into ancient biblical incidents.

Returning to the Bible, once Moses arrives at Mt Sinai, Downing again notices a possible UFO event. When Moses climbs the mountain to meet the Lord, is a UFO landing?

"And Mt Sinai was altogether on a smoke because the Lord descended upon it in fire; and the smoke thereof ascended as the smoke of a furnace, and the whole mount quaked greatly."
(*Exodus 19:18*)

When Moses climbs Mt Sinai to receive the tablets, he enters the cloud. Was he entering a UFO?

"Then Moses went up on the mountain, and the cloud covered the mountain. The glory of the Lord settled on Mount Sinai, and the cloud covered it for six days; and on the seventh day he called Moses out of the midst of the cloud. Now the appearance of the glory of the Lord was like a devouring fire on the top of the mountain in the sight of the people of Israel. And Moses entered the cloud."

Another *Old Testament* prophet, Elijah, may have had some UFO encounters. When he finishes his life on Earth he is in the company of his successor Elisha by the river Jordan:

"And it came to pass, as they still went on, and talked, that, behold, there appeared a chariot of fire, and horses of fire, and parted them both asunder; and Elijah went up by a whirlwind into heaven."
(*Kings 2:1-11*)

The theme of clouds can be found in other parts of the Bible. In his book *The Bible and Flying Saucers* Barry Downing states:

"It is important to notice that the 'cloud' tradition made some impression on later Hebrew literature. In the Psalms we find the 'pillar of cloud' is seen as a vehicle by which God travels - it is not God himself; 'lift up a song to him who rides upon clouds' (Psalm 68:4).

It is this same God who 'makest the clouds thy chariot' (Psalm 104:3); here is a possible link between the 'cloud' tradition of Moses and the 'chariot' tradition of Elijah. While the language is figurative, its origin in Hebrew tradition seems to be concrete, When Jeremiah wishes to speak about the mobility of God, he says, 'Behold, he comes up like clouds, his chariots like the whirlwind; his horses are swifter than eagles - woe to us for we are ruined' (Jeremiah 4:13) " [7]

In the *New Testament*, Downing found a number of possible UFO events. These are: **T**he Star of Bethlehem, The Baptism of Christ, The Transfiguration of Christ and The Ascension.

The Star of Bethlehem

This symbol has puzzled scholars for many years. Some have theorised it was a natural phenomenon such as a comet. Matthew records that the 3 wise men followed the star *"till it came to rest over the place where the child was."* (Matt 2:9). But as Downing says stars do not move and then suddenly stop. Likewise the same goes for the comet theory. Taking this into account a UFO is as valid as any other theory.

The Baptism of Christ

As Jesus was baptized it is stated in *Matthew (3:16-4:1)* *"And when Jesus was baptized, he went up immediately from the water, and behold, the heavens were opened and he saw the Spirit of God descending like a dove, and alighting on him; and lo, a voice from heaven, saying, "This is my beloved Son, with whom I am well pleased." Then Jesus was led up by the Spirit into the wilderness to be tempted by the devil."* Once again we have an object in the sky. This time it descends and then carries him away. In John's Gospel after the baptism sequence Jesus calls to Nathaniel and tells him *that he would "see heaven opened, and the angels of God ascending and descending upon the Son of man." (John 1:51)*. It therefore appears that Jesus had contact with beings from another world following his Baptism.

The Transfiguration of Christ

"Before Christ was crucified, Jesus together with disciples Peter, James and John went up a high mountain and Jesus was transfigured before them, and his face shone like the sun, and his garments became white as light. And behold, there appeared to them Moses and Elijah, talking with him, And Peter said to Jesus; "Lord I will make three booths here, one for you and one for Moses and one for Elijah." He was still speaking, when lo, a bright cloud overshadowed them, and a voice from the cloud said, "This is my beloved Son, with whom I am well pleased; listen to him." When the disciples heard this, they fell on their faces, and were filled with awe. But Jesus came and touched them, saying, "Rise and have no fear." And when they lifted up their eyes, they saw no one but Jesus only" (Matthew 17:1-8).

The cloud like object has made yet another appearance. Modern UFO accounts sometimes describe objects so bright the witnesses are unable to look directly at them.

The Ascension

In Jesus' last meeting with the disciples, we read:

"So, when they had come together, they asked him, Lord, will at this time restore the kingdom of Israel?" He said to them," It is not for you to know times or seasons which the Father has fixed by his own authority. But you shall receive power when the Holy Spirit has come upon you; and you shall be my witness in Jerusalem and in all Judea and Samaria and to the end of the earth. And when he had said this, as they were looking on, he was lifted up, and a cloud took him out of their sight. And while they were gazing into heaven as he went, behold, two men stood by them in white robes, and said, Men of Galilee, why do you stan-

Figure 14 (right):
The burnt vegetation from the 28th September visitation.
Figure 15 (far right):
An illustration of the craft etched into the beach and the pilot!
© Barry Chamish

Figure 16 (bottom right):
This image is called the Gilgal Refaim or 'Circle of Giants' located in the Golan Heights. It consists of five concentric rings, the largest of which is 159 metres. Archeologists are mystified by this structure. No other complex in the Middle East resembles it and it predates the pyramids by 500 years. It is not thought to have been constructed by local nomads but rather outsiders. Its function may have been to measure the rising of the star Sirius in 3000 BC. According to the Bible the only outsiders living on the Golan Heights back then were giants.

looking into heaven? This Jesus, who was taken up from you into heaven? This Jesus, who was taken up from you into heaven, will come in the same way as you saw him go into heaven." (Acts 1:6-11)

Reverend Downing suspects the Ascension cloud was the same UFO that guided the Israelites through the Red Sea, gave Moses the tablets, carried Elijah to heaven, 'descended' like a dove at the Baptism, carrying him into the Wilderness and bodily at the Ascension. This was also probably the same cloud, which appeared at the Transfiguration and may have been the Star of Bethlehem. [8]

DID THE GIANTS RETURN?

Moving forward into modern times one finds the land of Israel still has its fair share of UFO sightings. In fact in 1987 a major UFO flap started. On the evening of the 28th September 1987, 27-year-old Ami Achrai was dri-

ving south of Haifa in northern Israel when he saw a disc-shaped craft which emitted a bright red flash before disappearing. When Achrai returned to the scene two days later with Ufologist Hadassah Arbel , they were amazed to find a 15 metre ellipsoid disc burned into the sands of Shikmona Beach. In nearby vegetation was the image

purporting to show an image of the pilot of the craft facing a control board. When the sand was sent for analysis the results showed the particles were covered in a low-melting hydrocarbon material.

On the 9th June 1988, another image of a similarly shaped craft was etched into Shikmona beach. On the 27th April 1989, two teenagers claimed to have witnessed a UFO explode over the beach, leaving thousands of shards. The shards were found to consist of very pure magnesium, 6000 times higher than the surrounding area.

What is most interesting about these cases is that they occurred about 200 metres away from a biblical shrine called Elijah's cave. According to legend Elijah preached here. In this cave is an ancient drawing of what many claim is very similar to what was burned into the beach. Had the biblical giants returned? In early July 1993 in Rishon Letzion, two huge bald beings beamed themselves into an apartment belonging to Batya Shimon. They told her telepathically not to be frightened and then proceeded to float around her room, dusting her shelves with a yellow foul smelling powder. After a few minutes they beamed themselves outside. Apparently the next night a dozen giants visted Batya, arriving and leaving in the same ethereal manner! Later on in the book you will witness many religious paintings with what seem like depictions of UFOs. For more information on these strange occurrences in Israel please consult *Return of the Giants* by Barry Chamish. Book World Inc 2000.

ISLAM

As well as examining the Bible it is worthwhile examining the Koran as well for accounts of non-human beings. Islam, in fact, describes three distinct species of intelligent beings in the universe: Angels, Men and Jinns. Angels are high beings created of light. Men are created with bodies of clay - poetic language for physical bodies assembled from mineral and chemical elements of our Periodic Table. Jinns are described in the Koran as being created before man. Ufologist and editor of *Flying Saucer Review Magazine* Gordon Creighton mentions that *"some Jinns could be fully physical and what we call extraterrestrials, while other species of them have an altogether and finer sort of matter..."* Many Jinns are described as being devils or shaytans, others, however, in the Koran are described as positive in nature. Creighton summarised his findings on Jinns:

*They are normally invisible to humans.
*They can materialise in the physical world.
*They can change shape and appear in any sort of guise including animal.
*They can lie and deceive.
*They abduct or kidnap humans.
*They tempt humans into sexual intercourse and liaisons with them.
*They often snatch up humans and teleport or transport them.
*Throughout Arabian literature there have been people who have been in league with the Jinns (both good and bad.) They have endowed their human contact with psychic powers.

*The Jinns have tremendous powers of telepathic ability and can 'cast a glamour' over their human victims.[9]

Any student of alien abductions will find many parallels with these characteristics of the Jinns.

2) AFRICA

The Dogon Tribe

Figure 17) The Dogon's symbol of the Nommos (above):
© Ben Mason

The Dogons of Mali, are a remote tribe living in West Africa. What makes them unique is their advanced knowledge of the Sirius star system. The Dogon believe that a group of half-human half-amphibious 'gods' also called Nommos came from the Sirius system 5-6000 years ago, spending time among the Dogons imparting wisdom and knowledge. In Dogon art (see figure 17) the Nommos resemble the amphibian demi god Oannes in early Babylonian records and the Sumerian equivalent Enki. They say the Nommos first arrived from the Sirius system in a vessel that spun, or whirled, during its descent, accompanied by loud noises like roaring wind and skipped across the ground as it landed.

The Dogon cosmology revolves around the star called Po Tolo, meaning 'seed star', and this star is known to modern astronomers as Sirius B (discovered in 1862), the much smaller companion of Sirius A or Dog Star. The Dogon priests say that their knowledge about the Sirius system was passed down for many centuries orally and in secret, long before Westerners discovered them. Their knowledge extends to the orbiting period of Sirius B around Sirius A - 50 years- modern astronomy puts this figure at 50.04 years. They have also stated that Sirius B rotates on its own axis and takes one Earth year to do so. Interestingly, the Dogon's astronomical accuracy is not limited to the Sirius system. The Dogon priests also stated that Jupiter has four moons, that Saturn is encircled by a series of halo-like rings, that the planets orbit the sun, that Earth is round (not flat, as often alleged in primitive folklore), and that it rotates upon its own axis. They even spoke of the galaxy of stars, i.e. the Milky Way, being spiral in shape. Except for their Jupiter moon count, all of the Dogon's aforementioned claims are absolutely correct but none can be verified by scientific means without the assistance of complex instruments and/or calculations. And even their Jupiter moon count is not entirely incorrect, as only four are of significant size. Their apparently amazing knowledge was brought to the attention of westerners by two French anthropologists: Marcel Griaule and Germaine Dieterlen in the 1930's.

Some critics strongly doubt the validity of the Dogon's knowledge. In response to a book *The Sirius Mystery* written by Robert K.G. Temple in 1977 (with a more recent version, responding to the possible trinary nature of Sirius) astronomer Carl Sagan and many other critics said that modern knowledge of Sirius must have come from westerners who talked to the Dogon priests before the anthropologists arrived. Others say the French anthropologists themselves may have passed on their own astronomical knowledge to the tribe. Temple counters this by stating that the

Dogons also knew of the existence of Sirius C (mentioned in his 1977 book) but not discovered by astronomers until 1995. In a radio interview with Zoh Hieronimus Temple says:

"I made a daring prediction 20 years ago, based upon tribal information I analysed. I suggested that astronomers would eventually confirm the existence, in the system of the star Sirius, of a third star and that the third star would be a red dwarf. I'm delighted to point out that in 1995, two French astronomers, Benest and Duvent, published an article in Astronomy and Astrophysics, saying that they'd completed eight years of analysis of the perturbations in the Sirius system and they could confirm the existence of a third star, and it was a red dwarf." [10]

Other African Tribes

There are many other African tribes that describe the arrival of heavenly beings. Here are just a few examples:

- The Masai tribe tell the story of red, blue, white and black original gods who all came down from 'cloudland'.
- The Nandi tribe. Their chief God was called Tororut. He lived in heaven, was like humans but had wings, whose beating produced lightning and whose flapping was thunder. They also have another god named Chepkeliensokol. Translated this means 'the thing with the nine ray-legs'.
- The Bantu people talk of, *"The lightning lay packed in a special egg. The first mother received fire from it. The egg broke and from its two halves, came all visible things. The upper half turned into a tree mushroom and rose high up into heaven. The lower half remained behind."* [11]

South African Zulu shaman Credo Mutwa writes in his book *The Song of the Stars:*

"There are things that fly through the night, that you call UFOs, which we in Africa call Abahambi Abavutayo, 'the fiery visitors'... Long before they were heard of in other parts of the world, we, the people of Africa, had contact with these things and the creatures inside them. I can only speak within certain constraints because we are not allowed to talk in any detail about these sacred things. Our people fear that should we do that, then the star ships would stop visiting us."

Mutwa describes one type of being that sounds very familiar to those who have read abduction accounts. He calls it the Matindane, *"the grey or white ... creature with a largish head whose face is chalk-white, with large green eyes that go round the creature's head so that it can look at you over its shoulder..."* Mutwa goes on to say:

"These are creatures who are watching over us curiously, and who, I think, are

regulating human progress for some reason."

Probably the most sensational African UFO case in modern times is that which occurred at Ariel Primary School in Ruwa, South Africa on the 15th September 1994. Initially several school children spotted a cigar shaped object hovering in the sky. The next day was a day of incredible events. The children went outside for their morning break and were amazed to observe a purple light flashing in the sky followed by a large disc shaped object, which descended into a nearby empty field. The reactions of the children were mixed, some panicked and some were transfixed by the whole event. The commotion that followed attracted all of the kids in the playground and now around 100 children were observing the landed

Figures 18 & 19 (right):
Two of many sketches made by the children following their encounter
Source:
http://www.etcontact.net

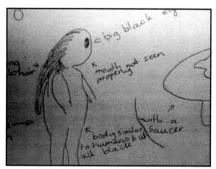

craft. After the craft landed several balls of light, or miniature discs flew around for a short time. Next, three beings emerged from the craft. One stood near the craft and the other two moved forwards. They were described as about 1.2 metres tall with black shiny tight fitting overalls. Two of them were bald while the third had long black hair. Their faces were described as dark, with large wrap around eyes with small noses and mouths. Some of the children described receiving telepathic images and messages concerning the Earth's environment. After this the beings returned to their craft which then began to flash and was gone in a burst of light. The startled children returned to the school building to inform their teachers of what had occurred. After listening to the children, some of whom were hysterical, the staff realised that what they were saying was true. This case was extensively investigated by Journalist Cynthia Hynd.

THE EGYPTIANS

According to Orthodox Egyptology, Egyptian society started in 3100 BC and ended in 332 BC. This was the 'Dynastic' period when successive Pharaohs - 32 in all, ruled Egypt. When one looks at the Great Pyramid and marvels at its precision it is hard to accept that this was built in 2500 BC, only 600 years after the Egyptian civilisation started. Could a society advance that much in 600 years to build such an amazing monument? Was there an earlier more advanced society? Well, maybe there was.
Manetho's *History of Egypt* together with other sources: the Palermo stone,

the Turin Papyrus and the Abydos King-list give information on earlier rulers. Researchers have divided this information into three distinct eras:
a) The first era, when the Neteru (or 'Gods') ruled the land of Egypt.
b) The second era, the Followers of Horus, the Shemsu Hor. This lineage continued up to the human Pharaoh called Menes.
c) The Dynastic Kings whose names are individually catalogued in King lists.

Most orthodox Egyptologists discount the first two eras as fiction. Manetho's writings tell of the whole Egyptian civilisation lasting 36,525 years, from the time of the Gods to the last dynasty of the mortal kings. Another source, Greek historian, Diodorus Siculus who visited Egypt in

Figure 20) The Papyrus of Hunefer from the Book of the Dead 1310BC (below): Are there any possible depictions or accounts of UFOs in Egyptology? Well the Hunefer Papyrus, housed in the British Museum, shows the Opening of the Mouth Ceremony and depicts the Pharaoh's trip into the afterlife. Part of this image depicts a curious rocket shaped object.

the First Century BC received a figure of 23,000 years from the priests and chroniclers he spoke to. He was informed *"At first Gods and Heroes ruled Egypt for a little less than 18,000 years... Mortals have been kings of their country, they say, for little less than 5000 years."* Were these early Egyptian rulers extraterrestrials? Maybe we'll never know the answer, but for myself and many others, the Great Pyramid stands as a legacy to some knowledge of precision and architecture that was inherited from some earlier mysterious source!

There is also an account of Horus using a 'winged disc' in which he gives battle to Seth.[12]

In the ancient Pyramid Texts we read that Egyptian King Pepi ascended:
"As an imperishable star; Flies who flies! He flies away from you, O men! He is no longer upon earth; he is in the sky! He rushes at the sky like a heron. He has kissed the sky like a falcon. He has leapt skyward like a grasshopper..."

Many, like myself, think, could there be a 'physical' connection between ET's and the array of hybrid Egyptian deities found in their art and sculptures?

3) NORTH AMERICA

Researcher Peter Freuchen, in his work titled the *Book of the Eskimos* recounts one of their stories:

"The first were much bigger than present-day men. They could fly with their magic house, and the snow shovels moved of their own accord and shovelled the

© *Erich Von Däniken*

snow alone. If the people of that age wanted different kinds of food, they simply went into their flying houses and flew to a new place. But one day someone complained about the noise that the flying houses made when they flew through the air. As the words of the complainant were very strong, the houses lost their ability to fly, and since then men are bound to one place with their houses... In those days snow could burn like fire and fire often fell from heaven. Nor was there any ice at that time."*

The Hopi Indians possess some interesting tales. Their first world was called Tokpela, meaning infinite space. Their creator was called Taiowa, and he dwelt here before creating man. His supreme law to the Hopis was that "Thou shalt not kill". According to the *Book of the Hopi* the following legend is told:

"In ancient times there was a battle for the Red City in the South. Wherever they came from, all the tribes were accompanied by Kachinas, beings who were reputed not to be of the 'fourth world', indeed, they were not men at all. Nevertheless, they always proved themselves to be protectors and advisors of the tribe and frequently helped them out of tricky situations with superhuman powers and arts. This was what happened in the Red City in the South when some Hopi tribes were suddenly attacked from all sides. With the speed of the wind, the Kachinas built a tunnel through which the Hopis were able to flee into the open behind enemy lines without shedding blood. When they said goodbye, the Kachinas said to the chieftans; "We are staying to defend the city. The time for the journey to our distant planet has not yet come!" [13]

The Paiute Indians from California recount a superior civilisation known as the Hav-Musuvs. They say they used 'flying canoes' which were silver in colour and had wings. They describe them as flying like eagles and

making a whirring noise. The Hav-Musuvs were also said to possess a strange weapon. A small tube like device that could stun their enemies, resulting in paralysis and a feeling akin to pins and needles. [14]

4) SOUTH AMERICA
The Kayapo Tribe of Brazil

The Kayapo tribe of Brazil, commemorate the event of their legend of the teacher from heaven (see figure 23). One could be forgiven for thinking the tribesman in costume is impersonating a spaceman. Could they be recreating the moment when ETs walked amongst primitive cultures imparting wisdom and knowledge? Researcher Joao Americo Peret visited the tribe and spoke with head of the clan Kuben Kran Kein. He relayed their legend:

Figures 22 (above):
Bep Kororoti

"Their god is called Bep Kororoti. He visited the village in ancient times wearing a bo (the straw suit seen in the picture) that covered him from head to foot. He carried a kop, a thunder weapon, in his hand. The villagers were scared at the presence of this strange being, some of the men of the village tried to attack Bep but their weapons turned to dust. He demonstrated the power of his kop by aiming it at a tree and then a stone, destroying them both. Eventually when the villagers realised he meant no harm they befriended him. He married a local lady and they had children. The daughter was named Nio Pouti. One day Bep went up into the mountains of Pukato Ti and vanished into thin air, surrounded by fiery clouds, smoke and thunder. Nio, his daughter, married and one day she took her husband up to Pukato Ti as she told him she knew where there was food for the whole tribe. She sat in a tree and asked her husband to bend the branches of the tree till the branches touched the ground. At that moment Nio disappeared amid clouds of dust and smoke and lightning. After waiting for several days, Nio's husband heard a crash and the tree reappeared with both Bep and Nio along with baskets of food, the likes of which he had never seen before. After a time Bep asked him to bend the branches of the tree down to the earth. There was an explosion and the tree disappeared again." [15]

The Incas

The Incas occupied Peru until the Conquistadors arrived in AD 1532. Their God was called Viracocha which means foam of the sea. He is traditionally depicted as a lean, elderly, bearded white man, wearing sandals and a long flowing cloak. He is certainly not like the dark indigenous population! His legacy seems to have been to travel around working wonders in science, engineering and also as a healer civilising the peoples and communities he came into contact with throughout the Andes. Some possible examples of his work exist in some of the Inca buildings, pyramids and temples built out of huge rocks weighing many tons and hewn together with amazing precision. Many people today wonder how on earth these blocks were moved around; maybe a clue lies in an ancient description which describes the huge blocks being lifted through the air to the sound of a trumpet. Another interesting story describes Viracocha as being accompanied by 'messengers' - faithful soldiers (huaminca) and 'shining ones' (hayhuaypanti). Their role being to carry their lord's message to every part of the world. Incan legends state that Viracocha eventually left and traversed by water, hence his title 'foam of the sea'. [16]

The Mayans

As we move north from the Andes into Mexico we come across the famous Mayan civilisation, renowned for its exquisite architectural achievements and astronomical knowledge. They are considered to be descended from the Olmecs. Very little is known about the Olmecs, but it is estimated that they flourished between 800 BC and 400 BC. The Mayans consequently followed from 300 BC to 900 AD. The Mayan Indians of Central America have a book entitled the *Popol Vuh* (not a genuine ancient book but one written in the 16th Century by an unknown Mayan.) This

Figure 23 (right):
This is a photograph of
the coffin lid of Mayan
King Pacal, Palenque.
AD *683. He seems to be*
sitting forward on some
device and operating
controls with his hands.
The object appears to
have exhaust fumes at
the rear. Archeologists
state that the image rep-
resents Pacal at the
moment of his death
descending into the
underworld.

Figures 24 & 25
(opposite):
These two photographs
are part of a sequence of
20 images taken by Snr.
Don Raul Dominiquez
Lopez as a UFO was
rising from a lake in
Ocotlan, State of Jalisco
on 24th April, 1993.

Could the 'Gods' of
the ancient South
American tribes have
travelled in objects
like the one opposite?

book mentions several Gods including Hunahpu, Xbalanque and Quetzalcoatl who returned to the stars after their life on Earth ended. The description of Quetzalcoatl bears a striking resemblence to Viracocha :

"A mysterious person... a white man with strong formation of body, broad fore-head, large eyes, and a flowing beard. He was dressed in a long, white robe reaching to his feet. He condemned sacrifices, except of fruits and flowers, and was known as the God of Peace. When addressed on the subject of war he is reported to have stopped up his ears with his fingers." [17]

According to the *Popol Vuh*, the Mayan's forefathers:

"Were endowed with intelligence; they saw and instantly they could see far; they succeeded in seeing; they succeeded in knowing all that there is in the world. The things hidden in the distance they saw without first having to move... Great was their wisdom; their sight reached to the forests, the rocks, the lakes, the seas, the mountains, and the valleys. In truth, they were admirable men... They were able to know all, and they examined the four corners, the four points of the arch of the sky, and the round face of the Earth." [18]

It also has a passage implying that humans were created to be the servants of the Gods:

"Let us make him who shall nourish and sustain us! What shall we do to be invoked, in order to be remembered on earth? We have already tried with our first creations, our first creatures; but we could not make them praise and venerate us. So then, let us try to make obedient, respectful beings who will nourish and sustain us." [19]

One can draw parallels with the Sumerian stories of modern man being created by these Gods.

There is an intriguing description of Quetzalcoatl's departure from Mexico:

"...He set sail on the Eastern sea preceded by his attendants who had been changed into bright birds." [20]

According to American anthropologist Brian Stross, the Tzeltal Indians from Mexico have legends of small black beings known as Ikals. They are described as being three feet tall, hairy and black in colour. Stross was informed that these beings were seen in both ancient and modern times, sometimes attacking or kidnapping Indians. Occasionally people had been paralysed when they encountered an Ikal. [21]

5) AUSTRALASIA
Papua New Guinea

In 1967, Stan Seers, author of the book *UFOs -The Case For Scientific Myopia* related an interesting story from the people of Papua New Guinea. It tells of the 'Greys' with strange heads that brought the local tribes to the land of New Guinea Highlands and who one day will come and take them back in life or in death. The current and accepted interpretation of the 'mud men' or 'grey men' history, body art and masks of clay is simply a local Papuan New Guinean response to death, by representing death as flaking skin of corpses. Their skin is coated with grey river mud for the effect and a heavy mask is made to cover the face.

Australia

The Aboriginal tribes of Australia base their creation around a concept known as the Dreamtime. According to their legends, there were many types of ancestral spirits back in that original epoch. Anthropologists today regard their stories of strange beings and animals as pure fantasy. The Aboriginals, however, regard them as fact. The Wiradjuri tribe from New South Wales talk of the Yuurii, who are described as little hairy men

Figure 26 (left):
We can draw parallels here with the Bep Kororoti story from Brazil. Tribes people attire themselves in costume or make up, re-enacting ancient events of the visitation of their creator Gods.
© Galen Fry Singer

and women no taller than 3 feet, with long fingernails and big teeth. The males have long beards also. The Gumbaingirr tribe call these tiny people the Bitarr. The Aboriginals from Victoria speak of other small beings. The Nyols, small stony-grey humanoid beings who inhabit caverns beneath the surface. Another type is the Netnets who have brown skin and long sharp claws. Another truly bizarre description is that of the Pot-koorok, a small frog-like humanoid with large webbed feet, long fingers and a pear shaped body. Old Red-Eye is a weird creature who is said to be able to materialise anywhere and mesmerise a person with its red eyes. Stranger still is the Yara-ma-yha-who, which is a tiny toothless frog-like man that has suckers on its hands. It is said that it likes to suck the blood of its victims! [22]

CHAPTER CONCLUSION

Having now read these various accounts of possible UFO and ET contact in the myths, legends and stories from cultures in ancient history, we are left asking ourselves why are there not more detailed accounts of UFOs in ancient times. Aside from the ancient Indian texts, information on ancient UFOs and non-human entities, is sparse. To answer this point we have to pay another visit back into history and look at the terrible destructions that took place of historical books and texts:

The Alexandria Library is considered to be the most complete and important library in history. Ptolemy I, a Macedonian Greek general under Alexander the Great, founded it near the end of the Fourth Century BC. It consisted of over half a million volumes of priceless works of science and literature. Unfortunately it was destroyed in AD 391 at the orders of Emperor Theodosius I under the advice of a bishop named Theophilos. It would be centuries before humankind could begin to reconstruct what was lost at Alexandria. In 1450, all of Europe only possessed a tenth of the books held at Alexandria! Other infamous destructions of libraries include:

- Destruction of the collected works of the Greek Emperor Pisistratus.
- Total destruction of the Egyptian library in the Temple of Ptah, Memphis.
- 500,000 volumes destroyed when the Romans invaded Carthage.
- Chinese emperor Tsin Shi Hwang-ti ordered the burning of all books in 213 BC.

One can only wonder, if none of the wanton destruction had occurred above, what knowledge and wisdom we would have today. Would we have a fuller and clearer picture of UFO visitation in history?

SOURCES

1) Richard L Thompson *Alien Identities – Ancient Insights into a Modern UFO Phenomenon,* Govardhan Hill Inc 1993. Richard Thompson's fascinating tome parallels modern UFO accounts with ancient Sanskrit writings of India.

2) Srimad Bhagavatam, *Sixth Canto,* Part 3

3) Srimad-Bhagavatam (Bhagavata Purana) - Bhaktivedanta Book Trust 1991. A virtual encyclopedia of yoga, meditation, and the mystic arts. It brings together in one complete source, information that previously took hundreds of books to explain. The Bhagavatam, with elaborate commentary, is the most widely read and authoritative translation available to the English-speaking world. *Canto One* through Nine as well as Chapters One through Thirteen of the *Tenth Canto,* are the product of the scholarly and devotional effort of His Divine Grace A.C. Bhaktivedanta Swami Prabhupada. After Srila Prabhupada departed from this world in 1977, his disciples completed the work by translating the balance of the *Tenth Canto,* along with the entire *Eleventh and Twelfth Cantos.*

4) Von Däniken, Erich; *Gold of the Gods.* pp141-148

5) Stonehill, Paul; *Mysteries of the Yellow Emperor. http://ufoinfo.com/news/yellowemp.html*

6) Alford, Alan; *Gods of the New Millennium. Hodder & Staughton 1998*

7) Downing, Barry; *The Bible and Flying Saucers. Shpere Books* 1968. p.91

8) Blumrich, Josef - *The Spaceships of Ezekiel. Bantam Books* 1974

9) Creighton, Gordon; *A Brief Account of the True Nature of UFO Entities,* FSR Vol 29 No5

10) Temple, Robert; *The Sirius Mystery.* Arrow , 1977
UFO Magazine UK May / June 1999 pp 68-70

11) Von Däniken, Erich; *According to the Evidence.* Souvenir Press. 1977 pp 97-100

12) *Egyptian Literature Vol 1* Wallis Budge.

13) Von Däniken, Erich; *Gold of the Gods.* Souvenir Press. 1973 pp 140-141

14) Vallee, Jacques; *Passport to Magonia.* Tandem. 1975 p 62

15) Von Däniken, Erich; *Gold of the Gods.* Souvenir Press. 1973 pp 145-150

16) Hancock, Graham; *Fingerprints of the Gods.* Century. 1995 pp 33-87

17) Ibid, 102

18) Ibid, 21

19) Delia Goetz and Sylvanus G Morley, *Popul Vuh,* the sacred book of the ancient Quiche Maya

20) Milton Joyce, Orsi, Robert and Harrison, Norman; *The Feathered Serpent and the Cross* Cassell London 1980

21) Vallee, Jacques; *Passport to Magonia.* Tandem 1975 p 61

22) P N Shuker, Dr Karl; *The Unexplained.* Carlton Books 1996 p 195-196

PREHISTORIC ARTISTS *Chapter Four*

The oldest forms of art are considered to be some 32,000 year old cave paintings from the Vallon Pont D'arc region in Southern France. Around this time, Cro-Magnon man came into being and lived in caves or in the shelter of overhanging rocks. On cave walls, particularly in South Western France, Spain and parts of Africa, are where we find the earliest paintings in the form of pictographs and petroglyphs. Pre-historic artist after artist added images on walls, until a cave might have hundreds of different paintings. Some of the art discovered exists quite deep within subterranean chambers, which, in the case of the Chauvet cave in France, were not discovered until 1993. Our Palaeolithic ancestors would have had to crawl on their bellies, through mazes of narrow, dark tunnels, by the light of a flickering torch or a spoon-like oil lamp, carrying the paints they had carefully prepared. Herds of reindeer and other large herbivores roamed the planet at that time and many of us are familiar with prehistoric paintings, depicting the hunting of bison with human figures and spears. Anthropologists posit that images of hunts were a form of ritual magic. It is theorised that by painting hunting scenes, 'primitive man' felt he would have killed an animal's vital spirit and therefore this act would lead to a successful kill. A popular misconception is that these early artists used charcoal to create these paintings. Actually, most art was not made with charcoal, but rather with mineral pigments, such as iron oxide (red ochre) or black manganese. They often drew stick figures for people, but the animals were well drawn and usually filled in with natural colours, to give them more shape and substance. On closer inspection of these works of art, however, not all is as it seems. As some of these wall paintings depict other strange objects not normally associated with the orthodox view of Palaeolithic cave paintings.

PART 1) STRANGE CRAFT

Our journey begins in Northern Tanzania with researcher Mary Leakey. Leakey, wife of famous anthropologist John Leakey catalogued over 600 paintings spanning over 180 sites. As well as the usual hunting scenes, which one would expect, Leakey found the humans in the paintings rather unusual and classified them into three categories:

The photograph on the opposite page was taken at the Great Gallery in Canyonlands National Park, Utah.

- The 'bushman', who are always faceless. Their heads are round, hips disproportionately large and they are very short.
- The second styles are called 'kolo' possessing elongated bodies, long hair, thumb-less hands and feet showing spurs.
- The third style shows extremely tall beings, sometimes up to one metre tall, always depicted in isolation.

After reading one of Leakey's publications, *Africa's Vanishing Art*, researcher JJ Benitez noticed some other anomalies in the images, including hat shaped objects (see figure 1), a figure in some kind of box or craft leaning over looking at an animal (figure 2) and some of the 'humans have four fingers and no thumbs. Benitez noted some pictures have several 'suns' in them - that is circles with lines beaming all around. The local tribes were asked in the 19th Century who created these images and they replied that it wasn't their ancestors. This begs the question, who painted

Figure 1 (right):
Notice the two disc
shaped objects
© Africa's Vanishing Art
Leaky

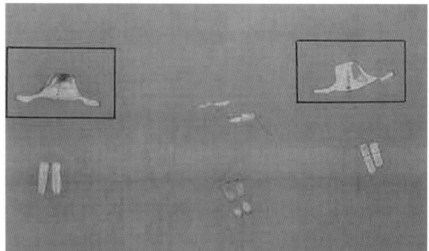

Figure 2 (right):
Notice the entity in the
far right of the picture.
He seems to be leaning
over looking at the ani-
mal from some kind of
box or craft (see detail
below.)

them and what was represented?

Using C-14 dating and date association to objects found at the foot of the rocky shelters: bones, eggshells, etc, the experts deduced that they were painted during a period spanning 50,000 - 16,000 years. Many went back to 29,000 years. If those painters copied the anatomy of both animals in such a perfect, meticulous way, what can we think of those other objects that seem so out of context?

A similar situation exists in the caves of Southern France (see figure 4 below). Located on the walls of the Pech Merle caves in Les Cabrerets, are a number of saucer- like shapes amongst more usual hunting scenes. They are dated to 15,000 BC.

We are used to seeing hunting scenes on these prehistoric cave paintings, as this was a predominant activity of Neolithic man. Why go to the trouble of painting such abstract shapes? Could they have been rendering what scientists refer to as entoptic imagery brought on through hallu-

Figure 3 (below):
This picture has a disc shaped object with lines running through it, four legs and two antennae like appendages.
© Africa's Vanishing Art Leaky

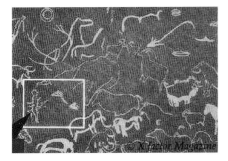

cinogenic plants? Or did our ancestors actually witness these strange creatures and objects? Both options are debatable.

Figure 4) The Wounded Man (left):
This image from Peche Merle is known as the 'Wounded Man'.
A figure can be discerned whose body has been pierced by a number of spears.
What is the curious hat shaped object in the top left of the image?

Figure 5) Strange Objects (right):
A French scientist named Remi Michel compiled this chart showing many strange objects. Note that some of the objects have landing legs; others have dots beneath them, possibly indicating some sort of energy field. The idea of ETs flying around in craft on our planet is highly unpalatable to orthodox science. Anthropologists tend to attribute these objects as being fertility symbols.

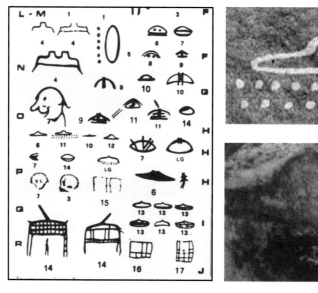

Figure 6 (right):
This is a sketch of a cave painting from the Varzelandia region, near the San Francisco river in Brazil. It was discovered by a Brazilian scientist named Araujo. The picture shows the Sun, Moon, a cigar shaped object and a flying saucer.

Figure 7 (top right):
The third picture depicts a classic saucer-like image. It was found in the Peche Merle caves in Les Cabrerets

Figure 8 (right):
Saucer shaped object found on a wall in Varzelandia, Brazil

7

8

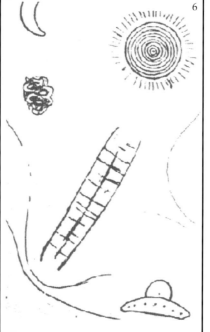

6

Figure 9 (Above:):
A 7000 year old petroglyph discovered in the Province of Queretaro, Mexico in 1966. In an almost prehistoric like scene from the film Close Encounters of the Third Kind, Four figures can be seen with their arms outstretched, below a large oval object radiating what appear to be beams of light.

The ancient Anasazi Indians in the American Southwest created these petroglyphs thousands of years ago. According to Indian folk-lore, two objects collided high in the sky and one crash-landed in the region of Death Valley. Some men arrived (presumably in another ship) and spent some time repairing the damaged craft and were observed by the local Indians. The two images at the top of the opposite page may possibly depict the ship used by the men who came to repair the damaged craft. In comparing the two images, the one on the right seems to depict structural damage around the edges and the bottom. Could it be the one

that allegedly crashed?

In 1977 researcher John Magor's published a fascinating book entitled *Our UFO Visitors*. In it a number of cave paintings were depicted from British Columbia, Canada. Some examples are shown below.

Figure 10 (below): *Shows a 2000 year old petroglyph from Nuevo Leon, Mexico. It is considered to be a picture of an Indian shaman, but to many it depicts a hat shaped object emitting beams of light or energy below. (Compare with the pair of hat shaped objects from Tanzania on page 68)*

Figure 11 (bottom left): *This photograph is of an Indian rock painting in Christina Lake, British Columbia. It measures 28 inches high and 31 inches wide. Judging by the calcite deposits and the rate of erosion of the red ochre that was used to draw it, it is considered to be 3000 years old. There are also two figures either side of the object, which seems to be standing on four legs.* © *John Magor*

Figure 12 (left): *More examples of cave art from Canada and Russia. The three examples are artists reconstructions. Two seem to resemble rockets. Compare the example from Kootenay Lake with an example of rock art from Navoi, Russia* © *Erich Von Däniken*

Cayuse Creek   Kootenay Lake   Navoi, Russia

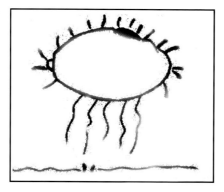

From looking at the examples in this first section, we have a common thread of flying objects depicted in ancient artworks from all around the world. Remember these examples are found in diverse locations, many years before the development of aircraft and hot air balloons .

PART 2) STRANGE BEINGS

As well as prehistoric art depicting aeriel craft, there are also many examples depicting exotic looking beings. There are quite a number where the entities are wearing some sort of protective head covering - almost similar to what an astronaut would wear. Others appear to wear close fitting suits or robes.

Figure14 (faright):
Photograph taken in Val Camonica, Italy and is dated to 10,000 BC.

The similarity between the Peruvian and the Italian example (above) is uncanny. Also, notice how both figures are depicted holding implements of some kind. Anthropologists state the halo like effect is the depiction of

Figure 15 (right, below & opposite page):
The first example (right) depicts a petroglyph from Toro Muerto, Peru, dated 12 -14,000 years old. All of these petroglyphs depict strange figures and the image below shows one with a curious object to it's left. Could these images be of UFOs? The first example is from Toro Muerto, Peru and the second (opposite page top left) from the southwestern region of the Mojave Desert.
© Erich Von Däniken

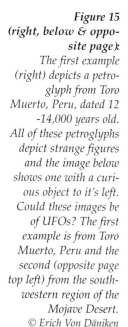

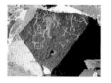

antlers being worn on the heads of the figures in ceremonial costume.

Other reasons for the 'luminous' halo/head gear equates to more esoteric symbolism found in numerous myths and religious texts.

The Tassili Culture of the Sahara region of Africa existed around 6000 BC and left behind a collection of over 4000 images of cave art, painted in a variety of colours. Many images depict scenes of hunts, battles and everyday life. What is of particular interest, however, are the images discovered by the 19th Century French explorer Henri Lhote. In the Djebel Zenkekra region, he discovered several hundred strange looking one-eyed figures with round heads. So strange in fact he called them Martians!

Two examples are shown below. These one-eyed creatures certainly do not look human. The figure on the left (figure 16) has four fingers and the 'being' on the right (figure 17) seems to have a UFO hovering behind it. Anthropologists have suggested that the Tassili 'roundheads' depict ceremonial dancers or priests wearing empty gourds over their heads.

Ufologist Gordon Creighton in his article *The one eyed entities of Belo Horizonte* (*Flying Saucer Review Magazine*) describes an alleged contact with one-eyed beings in Brazil, which occurred in August, 1963. The same beings were described as about ten feet in height and appeared to be wearing divers suits. They had a transparent helmet and one large, dark, round eye. Perhaps just a curious coincidence that they resemble Lohte's Martian God.[1]

One area, which has a rich source of peculiar looking entities in prehistoric artwork, is Australia. The first Aboriginal people are believed to have arrived in what is now Australia 40,000 to 50,500 years ago. Aboriginal religion

Figure 17 (below):
This cave painting is 18ft high! and was named the 'Great Martian God' by its finder Henri Lohte.

© *Erich Von Däniken*

Figure 18 (below):
These robed figures are from Sego Canyon, Utah. Estimated up to 5500 BC.

© *Source: www.indra/~dheyser/rockart.html*

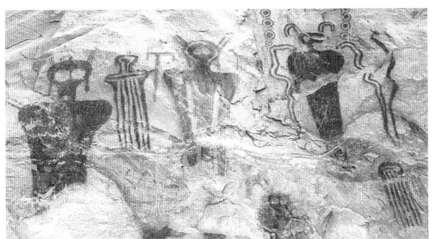

involves a number of deities who, according to their mythology, sent their sons to Earth to create and care for humanity. Aboriginal myths incorporate the idea of 'sky-beings', with the Wandjina among the most interesting to consider. The Wandjina have been preserved in a fascinating oral tradition and in a large collection of rock paintings scattered throughout the Kimberley region of northern Australia.

The illustrations on this page are from a book by Lt. Grey: *Journals of Two Expeditions of Discovery in Northwest and Western Australia 1837, 1838, & 1839*, held at Cambridge University Library. He led an expedition in the 19th Century to some caves near the Glenelg River region of Kimberley, Northern Australia. Exploring among hills near the Prince Regent River, Grey's party found a number of caves in which some extraordinary figures were painted. Were these representations of the 'deities' that came down in their original creation stories? Describing the main painting in the second cave Grey investigated, he wrote in his journal that:

"It was the figure of a man, ten feet 6 inches [3.2 metres] in length, clothed from the chin downwards in a red garment, which reached to the wrist and ankles... The face and head of the figure were enveloped in a succession of circular bandages or rollers ... these were coloured red, yellow and white: and the eyes were the only features represented on the face. Upon the highest bandage or roller, a series of lines were painted in red, but ... it was impossible to tell whether they were intended to depict written characters, or some ornament for the head." [2]
(See figures 19 & 20)

Figures 19 & 20) The Wandjina (below):
© Cambridge University Library
By permission of the Syndics of Cambridge University Library

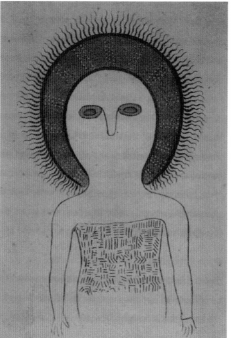

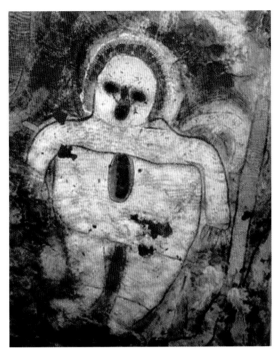 

Here are more examples from Kimberley, Australia, dated to 5000 BC. The textbook answer to these oddities is that they are the result of dream-like shamanistic experiences. The shaman would go into a trance-like state in order to contact 'spirit worlds' to procreate the spirits of the animals about to be killed by the tribal hunters, or to contact 'spirit ancestors'. They would then paint their entopic images on walls, objects for ceremonial purposes and everyday utensils.

The normal method of obtaining this state would be through the consumption of plant hallucinogens. The plants used would depend on the location, for example, Siberian Shamans would eat the Fly Agaric mushroom (Amanita Muscaria). Mexican Shamans would consume Peyote Cactus (Lophophora Williamsii). Other methods of inducing a trance -like state would be through the use of hypnotic drum beats, fasting, dancing and chanting. I have no doubt that some of the imagery we see on these old walls is the result of Shamanism. However, some of the imagery is common in style and subject across various areas of the planet, which may also be a common depiction of a specific extraterrestrial race - one that has interacted with various indigenous tribes?

There are a number of Aboriginal stories mentioning possible ET contact. According to the Bundjalung tribe of NSW there is the tale of the female ancestral being called Gaungan. Described as *"tall and slim, with flowing hair, beautiful hands and long fingernails,"* when she moved between Salty Lagoon and Wardell, Gaungan often appeared as a 'shining light'. An Aboriginal tribe called the Bad, from West Kimberly, Western Australia possess as part of their belief system a supreme being known as Djamar. According to their tradition the young initiates of the tribe were

Figures 21 & 22 (above): The Wandjina.

© *Kim Akerman*

led to a stony bed and shown holes where Djamar had planted his 'bull-roarer.' In Aboriginal lore the sound of the bullroarer (a roaring wind noise) symbolised the approach of the Gods.

E A Worms stated in *Djamar, the Creator Antropos XLV,1950* that:

"Earnestly the old men impress on the youths the terrible force of the original tjurunga (sacred stone), by pointing out the baldness of the surrounding hills and the damaged bark of the trees struck by Djamar when he whirled the bull-roarer. It smashed the rocks of the foreshore." [3]

One could interpret this lore as though Djamar landed in an object, damaging the surrounding landscape. The story ends with him ascending once again into the sky with his 'tjurunga'. Aboriginal Shaman A P Elkin mentions:

"Amongst the powers of the Mara medicine-men is that of climbing at night by means of a rope invisible to ordinary mortals up to the sky, where he can converse with the star people." [4]

Figure 23 (below left):
Taken at the Great Gallery in Canyonlands National Park, Utah.

Figure 24 & 25 (below right & top of opposite page):
Both images are etched into Nazca, South America. Both are 20+ metres in height.
© All photographs courtesy of:
www.daniken.com.

There are a number of remarkable similarities between depictions of these figures in rock art all across the world. For example, look at the creatures photographed in the Nazca landscape in Von Daniken's Arrival of the Gods, and two 'beings' portrayed on cave paintings from Australia. Notice how both pairs have antenna-like protrusions from their heads, coincidence?

Figure 26 (above):
Another example from Australia. This entity appears to have a tail and a zip up the front of its clothing! Was the artist trying to convey some sort of energy emanating from the being by drawing a line around it? Also, what is the object to the left of this figure?

Figure 27 (left):
Rock art from Australia. Notice the similarity with the Nazca figures, ie, round eyes, antennae and the large footwear on figures 25 and 27.

© *All photographs courtesy of Erich Von Däniken www.daniken.com*

Figure 30 Sumerian Heads (top right on opposite page):
These objects were found in Iraq and seem to have a reptialian appeerence.

Reptilian Figures in Iraq

If we examine old texts there is a recurring theme of Reptoid-like beings in all of the world's myths and legends.

In the Garden of Eden one finds the tale involving the serpent and in the ancient Jewish text the Haggadah, the serpent is described as being human-like in form. One text reads:

"He stood upright on two feet, and in height he was equal to the camel..." [5]

In the Zoroastrian (pre-Islamic Persian) cosmogony, Azidahaka, the serpent-demon defeats Yima, the first mortal, cutting him in two. In Egyptian mythology the Goddess Sati was a snake who preyed upon the dead and the adversary of Ra was Apep, the cosmic serpent. He chased Ra through the skies, eventually conquering him in the evening. In Norse/Teutonic mythology, at the root of the world tree, Yggdrasil, is the serpent Nidhog who's gnawing at its roots makes its stability uncertain.

In the *Enuma Elish*, the Babylonian creation epic there is a huge dragon named Tiamat who is the personification of the ocean and chaos and the mother of all that exists, including the Gods. She is an uncontrollable creature made of 'formless primordial matter.' [6]

Depictions of reptiles appear in figurines belonging to the ancient civilisation of Southern Iraq called the Ubaid. This very advanced culture is said to have commenced around 5000 BC. It was named after Tell al'Ubaid, the area where these figurines were first discovered during excavations by archaeologist Sir Leonard Woolley in 1922. He discovered reptilian looking figurines in the graves of the dead. It seems that the fig-ures were predominantly female with slim bodies, broad shoulders and lizard like heads (see figure 28). One depicts a female suckling a young offspring. Scholars believe these lizard figures are representations of the universal Mother Goddess - but not all are female.

Modern day ET abduction researchers occasionally receive descriptions of lizard-like entities from the abductees they work with.

According to Joe Lewels, PhD, in *The Reptilians: Humanity's Historical Link to the Serpent Race*, he says:

"John Carpenter has kept close track of the abduction phenomenon. He is the director of abduction research for the Mutual UFO Network (MUFON), one of the largest and most credible organizations dedicated to the scientific study of UFOs and abductions. Carpenter holds a master's degree in social work and is a highly qualified hypnotherapist who works as a psychiatric social worker in Springfield, Missouri. Since the late 1980s, he has worked with more than 100 abductees and compiled information on hundreds of others. In addition, he is in contact with other researchers in the field. He has been involved in ten cases where individuals have described reptilian entities and he is aware of researchers in other parts of the country with similar cases. Abductees often have distinct claw like cuts and bruises on their bodies after their apparent abductions! "

Carpenter summarised what he knows of these beings in his regular column, *Abduction Notes, MUFON UFO Journal*, April 1993: he says:

"Typically, these reptilian creatures are reported to be about six to seven feet tall, upright, with lizard like scales, greenish to brownish in colour with claw like, four-fingered webbed hands.... Their faces are said to be a cross between a human and a snake, with a central ridge coming down from the top of the head to the snout. Adding to their serpent like appearance are their eyes which have vertical slits in their pupils and golden irises."

30

Perhaps the most frightening and most controversial part of these stories are claims that the creatures occasionally are reported to have sex with abductees. Interestingly, some early artists would depict the biblical serpent as a bipedal figure. An example of this is shown (right) in this 15th Century Flemish painting by Hugo van der Goes. Later artists superseded this image with the familiar limbless snake.

CHAPTER CONCLUSION

All in all, I feel that these artworks, along with the thousands of experiences recorded by individuals in the last five decades, adds weight to the concept of UFOs and ETs visiting mankind thousands of years ago. How many more ancient depictions exist awaiting discovery, all adding another piece to this 'mind blowing' jigsaw puzzle?

Hugo van der Goes Diptychon mit Sündenfall und Erlösung (Beweinung Christi) linke Flügellinnenseite: Sündenfall
© Kunsthistorisches Museum, Wien oder KHM, Wien

SOURCES

1) *Flying Saucer Review,* an international quarterly magazine established in 1955. Long-term subscribers include overseas governments, air force libraries and Prince Philip. It is produced in England with the collaboration of more than seventy experts and specialists from Britain and twenty other countries, including Western Europe, and the USA, Canada, Latin America, Russia, Ukraine, Slovenia, China, Japan and the Middle East. They include numerous PhDs, doctors of medicine, astronomers, physicists and other scientific experts. It's editor is Gordon Creighton. *http://www.fsr.org.uk/fsrmain.htm*

2) Grey, George, Sir. *Journals of Two Expeditions of Discovery in North-West and Western Australia, During the Years 1837, 38, and 39,* under the authority of Her Majesty's Government ... with observations on the moral and physical condition of the Aboriginal inhabitants etc. London: T. and W. Boone, 1841. State Library of South Australia.

3) E A Worms stated in *Djamar, the Creator Antropos* XLV,1950, pp 643-658

4) Bill Chalker - *Australian Aboriginal Culture and Possible UFO Connections.* *http://www.project1947.com/forum/bcabor.htm*. Bill Chalker is one of Australia's leading UFO researchers and has written extensively on the subject. He is a contributing editor for the *International UFO Reporter*, the official publication of the US Centre for UFO Studies, CUFOS, and coordinates the NSW UFO INVESTIGATION CENTRE (UFOIC). He was the Australian representative for the Aerial Phenomena Research Organisation (APRO) from 1978 to 1986, and NSW state representative for the Mutual UFO Network (MUFON) from 1976 to 1993. In August, 1996, his book *The OZ Files - The Australian UFO Story* was published by Duffy & Snellgrove, Sydney.

5) The word Haggadah comes from the Torah command - *"And you shall tell (v'Higadeta) your children on that day..."* The earliest written Haggadah from 8th or 9th Century Palestine was found in the Cairo genizah, (a repository for discarded or worn sacred writings). The Haggadah is the story of the birth of the Jews as a people. It deals primarily with the events in Egypt that led from slavery to liberation, though it also spans the entire period from Abraham to the giving of the Torah at Mount Sinai.

6) *The Concise Oxford Dictionary* 7th ed 1982 s.v. 'Chaos'
Enuma Elish, "when the skies above. . .", is one of the oldest written creation myths in existence. Often compared to the biblical tale of *Genesis*, the earliest tablets date from around 2000 BC, although scholars feel that it was an ancient oral tradition before then The *Enuma Elish* is the Babylion creation epic and tells the tale of the creation of the universe, and of man himself. It is an epic tale of war and conquest, and was recited on the fourth day of the New Year's Festival that occurs around the Vernal Equinox.

UFOs IN WESTERN RELIGIOUS ART

H aving examined prehistoric artwork, it is now time to turn our attention to artworks from the medieval, Renaissance and post-Renaissance periods. Exclusively all of the artwork in this chapter depicts various religious scenes. As the majority of art from these time periods was religious in nature, inferences between UFOs and religion shouldn't be drawn too strongly from this connection. It is also important to bear in mind that these artworks would have been commissioned by wealthy individuals or organisations and there would have been strict limits as to what the artist would create and incorporate into his work. A wealthy person could take an artist into his or her household and in return the artist would supply the patron artistic needs, or someone or some organisation could commission a single work from an artist and employ him until that work was completed. In medieval times, most patronage came from the Church but the ruling classes, the kings, princes and nobles, made up a second group of patrons. These two systems of patronage continued during the Renaissance, along with the newer systems. Once the patron had chosen an artist, it was usual for the two of them to draw up a formal contract, setting out the specifications in some detail. In the early Renaissance, the patron had had the upper hand in such arguments, but as the status of artists rose they became less willing to be dictated to in matters of art. Sometimes it was agreed that the artist would accept advice from experts where necessary. As certain artists lacked a classical education, scholars would be called in to provide mythological and historical information. These 'scholars' were often members of secret societies and artists such as Leonardo da Vinci were prominent members of clandestine groups who had access to knowledge, esoteric systems, ancient maps and technologies outside of the public domain.

 Why do we find UFOs in these paintings? Perhaps we'll never know the answer. All one can do is to draw up a list of possibilities: firstly, the artist may have had a UFO sighting, secondly a friend or colleague may have had a sighting and relayed it to the artist, thirdly one cannot rule out the concept of matters relating to the occult. With this notion the artist may have been influenced by outside intelligences. Fourthly, in painting these out of place objects, the artist may have been influenced by a scholar in mythology impinging his ideas of expression into the mind of the artist and, lastly, it may just be sheer coincidence that the imagery painted by

The painting on the opposite page is
The Annunciation, with Saint Emidius, *by Carlo Crivelli. 1430 to 1495*

© *Courtesy of the National Gallery London*

Figure 1)
The Virgin Mary and
Saint Giovannino -
School of Lippi
1406-1469 (right):

One of the most out-
standing examples of
what looks like a UFO
in a historical artwork
is on display at the
Palazzo della Signoria
or Palazzo Vecchio,
Florence, Italy. This
enigmatic 15th Century
painting is known as
The Virgin Mary and
Saint Giovannino.
Catalogued as artwork
number 00292620 by
an unknown Florentine
author and originating
from the abandoned
Sant'Orsola monastery.
It has been attributed to
several artists including
Domenico Ghirlandaio,
Sebastiano Mainardi
and Jacopo del Sellaio,
but it is generally con-
sidered to originate
from the Florentine
painter Fra Filippo
Lippi (1406-1469)
or his school.[1]

© Courtesy Palazzo
Vecchio Italy

the artist has a remarkable similarity to what people would refer to today as a UFO. Enjoy this unique gallery of artwork and next time you look at a painting have a look in the sky!

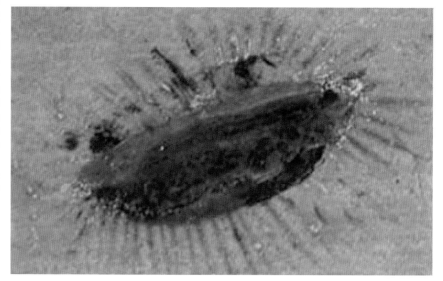

The painting first came to the attention of Ufological circles in November 1978 in an article entitled *La Madonna del disco volante* by Tuscan architect and researcher Daniele Bedini published in Italian UFO magazine *Notiziario UFO*. Bedini had noticed the unusual object in the painting whilst viewing it at the Palazzo Vecchio.[2]

One's eye is initially drawn to the figures in the foreground, the Virgin together with baby Jesus and Saint Giovannino. On further examination, however, one notices a curious object hovering at an angle in the sky.

Further enlargement (opposite) shows an oval or discoid craft with radiating gold spikes of light painted around its perimeter. This enlargement demonstrates the artist has gone to great lengths to portray this object as emanating luminescence. Further confirmation of this object is given by the presence of a man and his dog in the background, who appear to be looking up at the object. One wonders why the artist inserted this out of place object in the painting. Quite possibly he may have had a UFO sighting in his day and wished to relay this to others and to future generations.

As stated earlier, this painting is attributed to the school of Lippi. As a child, Fra Filippo was placed by his widowed mother in the monastery of Santa Maria del Carmine in Florence, where he received training as a painter and took religious vows as a monk in 1421. His early works were highly influenced by the earlier Florentine master, Masaccio. After 1440, Fra Filippo gradually abandoned Masaccio's precepts in favour of a more decorative style that recalled the Gothic in its use of fluttering draperies, attenuated figures, and glowing colours. He stressed the human aspects of his scenes; his Madonnas are sweetly pious or appealingly pretty (although sometimes lacking the spirituality of Madonnas by other painters), and his depictions of the Christ child and of cherubs are often playful or mischievous. In the famous *Madonna and Child* (1455, Uffizi Gallery, Florence), for instance, a boy angel grins out of the painting directly at the viewer. Much of this informality undoubtedly derives from his renunciation of his vows and subsequent marriage in 1461. The painter Filippino Lippi was his son. In later works, he combined traditional Gothic landscape elements with the new perspective style to create mysterious, receding backgrounds for his works.

Fra Filippo exerted a strong influence on later Florentine art. His style led directly to that of the Florentine painter Sandro Botticelli and the influence of his Gothic settings can be seen in Leonardo da Vinci's *Madonna of the Rocks*. He died in Spoleto on October 9, 1469.

This image received worldwide attention in 1996, when it was included in a 168 page Briefing Document authored by Don Berliner and funded by Laurence Rockefeller. The document deals with the many aspects of Ufology: the government cover-up and historical cases of UFO sightings around the world. The intention behind this project was to compile the 'best evidence' cases and dispatch the publication to heads of state around the world, including Bill Clinton. A thousand copies were printed and distributed but it has since been published commercially in paperback.[3]

The Annunciation - Carlo Crivelli 1486

This artwork was painted in 1486. In 1996 an engineer named Fabrizio Colista brought it to the attention of the Italian UFO community for reasons we shall read about shortly. The painting was initially held in the church of the Annunciata in Ascoli, Italy. In 1846, Lord Taunton presented it to the National Gallery in London, where it now resides as entry number NG739.

Figure 2)
The Annunciation,
with Saint Emidius,
by Carlo Crivelli.
1430 to 1495 (above
See page 84)
© *The National Gallery*
London

The town of Ascoli was under papal rule and in 1482 Pope Sixtus IV granted it a degree of self-government. This altarpiece was painted for the church of SS. Annunziata in Ascoli to celebrate the event. The coats of arms are those of the Pope (bottom left) and the local bishop, Prospero Cafferelli (bottom right). News of Ascoli's new status reached the town on the feast of the Annunciation on 25 March, which then became a special feast day when the town celebrated its liberty. It is rare to include a saint with the Archangel Gabriel in a depiction of the Annunciation. Saint Emidius, the patron saint of Ascoli, is shown carrying a model of the town. Ascoli is dominated by towers and is still recognisable today in the model which Emidius carries.
Inscribed: LIBERTAS.ECCLESIAS-TICA [Freedom of the Church].[4]

Crivelli was born in Venice, son of the painter Jacobo Crivelli, and received his early training in the Vivarini studio before moving to Padua, where he received his decisive impressions by working within the circle surrounding the workshop of Francesco Squarciones and studying the early works of *Mantegna*.
In 1457 he was sentenced to six months imprisonment for kidnapping a sailor's wife. In 1459, Crivelli left Italy and lived for some time in Dalmatia, present Croatia. On his return, he stayed in the province of Marches where he lived from 1468 until he died. Working in the province he mainly painted altarpieces for churches. Meeting the conservative tastes of his sponsors, he tried to preserve the Gothic tradition, even reintroducing the old gold background.

His pictures are characterised by a static, solemnity, primitive attitude to space (flat space) and strict linear drawing. Only precise and clean drawing of the faces, free disposition of fruit and flower garlands show that Crivelli was a painter of the early Renaissance in Italian art. The wood panels with St. Catherine of Alexandria, St. Peter, and Mary Magdalene from the Church of Santa Lucia in Montefiore dell'Aso in Italy

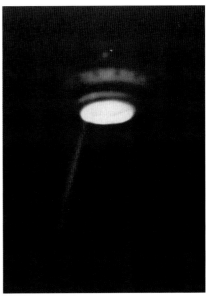

is characteristic of his style: sharply-angled, modelled figures clad in stiff-textured garments, and delicately painted faces, jewels and ornaments.[5]

Compare the Crivelli object with this photo (above right) taken by Ed Walters in Florida in 1987:

In the painting by Crivelli there is an enhancement of this UFO-like object. It appears to be constructed of several golden rings. Crivelli paints a long, pencil thin, laser like yellow ray shooting out from this unidentified flying object. The ray enters the building on the right, passes through the Holy Spirit (the dove) and then strikes the head of the Virgin Mary. What was the artist trying to portray in the painting? A flying object akin to a UFO with a beam of light striking a religious figure on the ground. Over the years there have been many eye witness accounts of flying objects and beams of light. Might Crivelli have been an observer of one of these occurences?

To conclude, the picture depicts a classical religious scene, that of Angel Gabriel making the annunciation to the Virgin Mary set within the town of Ascoli. The 'UFO' may well be religious symbolism but one may ask oneself what inspired the artist to paint something so familiar in form to what many people today regard a UFO.

Figure 3)
A photo of a UFO taken by Ed Walters, Gulf Breeze Florida on the 2nd December 1987 (above):
The photo has been light blasted and enhanced for detail.
Walter reported being hit by the blue beam.[6]
© Ed and Francis Walters

La Tebaide - Paolo Uccello 1460-1465

Another intriguing picture is *La Tebaide* by Paolo Uccello (*nee Paolo di Dono*), 1397-1475. It was painted towards the latter period of the artist's life c.1460-1465. It is housed at the Gallery of Academy in Florence, catalogue number 13971475. Florentine painter Uccello was one of the most distinctive artists of the early Renaissance. Vasari says he got his nick-

name (uccello means 'bird') because he loved animals, and birds in particular, and to his contemporaries, as well as to many later critics, he appeared an eccentric figure.

He is first documented 1412 in the workshop of the sculptor Ghiberti, but he is not known to have worked as a sculptor himself. In 1425 he

moved to Venice, where he worked as a mosaicist, but nothing survives there that can be certainly associated with him. By 1432 he was back in Florence, and in 1436 he painted his first dated surviving work - a huge fresco in Florence Cathedral depict-

Figure 4) The Tebaide (above):
© Courtesy of the Gallery of the Academy in Florence

ing an equestrian statue, a monument to the English condottiere Sir John Hawkwood (died 1394). It demonstrated the fascination with perspective that was central to his style.

His two other large-scale works are a series of frescos on *Old Testament* themes (probably 1430s and 1440s), in the 'Green Cloister' of Santa Maria Novella and a series of three panels (c1455) on the Battle of San Romano, a minor Florentine victory against the Sienese in perspective (1432). The pictures were painted for the Palazzo Medici and are now separated, with one panel each in the National Gallery, London, the Louvre, Paris, and the Uffizi, Florence.

Uccello's work presents a striking - and often captivating - combination of two seemingly opposing stylistic currents: the decorative tradition of International Gothic and the scientific involvement with perspective of the early Renaissance. Vasari maintained that Uccello wasted his time 'on the finer points of perspective' and presents him as an amiable fanatic who worked into the night and when told to come to bed by his wife would reply: *"What a sweet mistress is this perspective!"* Uccello's name became so identified with the subject of perspective that he was often said to have invented it.[7]

Depicted in *La Tebaide* is a series of religious episodes arranged in pattern; thus the viewer starts from bottom right moving towards the left and upwards. The scenes refer to different religious circles, for example, the Franciscans, Servitas, Camaldoleses and Cistercians, each represent various divisions of monastic experience. Our attention is drawn to the crucifixion scene in the centre of the painting.

The red disc-shaped object with a dome feature can clearly be seen in this enhancement. The brush strokes (to the left of the object) appear to indicate movement. In this artwork, Paolo Uccello has painted a red disc-shaped object with a dome on top hovering between the tops of some pine trees (see figure 4). Once again we have a historical painting with a UFO present. The detractors of the Ufological hypothesis state this object is nothing more than a cardinal's hat. Pope Innocenzo IV introduced this hat in about 1245. It had two tassels or fiocchi on the brim and ten suspended on each side from cords. Is it a hat or UFO? That is the question we may never know the answer to?

Figure 5) The Life of the Virgin Mary (below):

© *Notre-Dame Collegiate of Beaune, France.*

The Life of the Virgin Mary 15th Century

The eyes of an attentive observer will be struck by *The Life of the Virgin Mary* and *la Magnificat,* two medieval tapestries, which are part of a group of five depicting scenes from the Virgin Mary's Life. They were woven in the 15th Century in Tournai, Belgium and are now housed in the Notre-

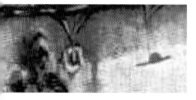

Dame Collegiate of Beaune, France. In both these tapestries there is an unidentified flying object hanging in the sky. The author of this book contacted the Notre-Dame Collegiate and was informed that they were of the opinion that the 'UFOs' were priests hats. But why spoil an expensive and time-consuming artwork by inserting a large black hat?

Figure 6)
la Magnificat (right):
© *Notre-Dame Collegiate*
of Beaune

Summer's Triumph- Anon 1538

This curious tapestry depicts symbolically the season of summer. More than likely, one of a series of four depicting the seasons. This tapestry is listed as item number L 71/45 and is on display at the

Figure7)
Summers Triumph
(below):
© *Leih - Diapositiv bitte*
Zurück an Bayerisches
National Museum

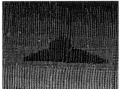

Bayerisches National Museum in Munich, Germany. Little information is known about the artwork other than it was purchased from an art dealer in 1971. The artist is listed as anonymous. The date "1538" is woven into the border on both the right and left side of the tapestry. In the upper border there is an inscription in old Latin "REX GOSCI SIVE GUTSCMIN". This translates as "King Gosci of Gutscmin."[8] As usual, for the context of this chapter, several disc- shaped objects are visible in the sky in the background. The artist does not appear to try to conceal them, as there are at least four in the picture.

Glorification of the Eucharist by Bonaventura Salimbeni 1595

Figure 8)
Glorification of the Eucharist (below):
© *Courtesy of Church of Saint Peter, Montalcino*

A Renaissance painting from 1595 ascribed to Bonaventura Salimbeni (1567-1613) resides in the church of Saint Peter in Montalcino, near Florence, Italy. The Sienese painter, Bonaventura Salimbeni, at the end of the 1500's, was awarded a commission for a work to be executed for the right hand altar of the Church of San Pietro at Montalcino. His work was to be completed for the year 1600 because the commission was to commemorate the Christian Jubilee that year. The painting has been signed: *Ventura Salimbeni/pittorserenis/fecit/anni jubilei/1600.*

This wonderful piece of art is structured vertically and the Holy Eucharist is placed in the geometric centre, surrounded by various holy people and priests on each side. In the upper part of the painting, the Holy Trinity is depicted: On the right is God the Father, on the left is God the Son, and above them in the centre, is the Dove which represents the Holy Spirit. In the lower left, one of the people wears a

crown similar to that of a Pope. Many believe it to be Pope Clemente VII.

One quickly notices the strange spherical object sitting between God the Father and God the Son, directly below the Dove. It is most accurately described as a shining, metallic coloured sphere with a strange glow rising at the top. The globe itself is coloured in various shades of grey and green and banded by horizontal and vertical lines. Some researchers feel they resemble a rough sketch of the Earth's meridians, others feel they resemble metallic welding.

There are also two long, straight rods attached to the surface of the sphere. The rods appear to widen at the bottom to form a round base on the sphere, while at the very tips of the narrow end of the rods. One can see a cross on the one and a vertical line on the other - possibly representing positive and negative polarities. One wanders whether these rods are some kind of antennae, as both God the Father and God the Son are holding them. One notices a small, round tube-shaped protrusion at the bottom left of the sphere. It looks remarkably like a telescope or possibly even a video camera! This painting has baffled Ufologists for decades, as this sphere is uncannily reminiscent of early satellites launched into space during the 1950's (For example, the US Vanguard II satellite launched by the USA in 1959). This painting was put to canvas in the year 1600. What did Bonaventura Salimbeni see in the skies above Sienese territory more than four hundred years ago? What on Earth - or in space - prompted him to

depict the Holy Trinity in this strange manner? Maybe the fact that many of the Renaissance masters had access to an underground stream of knowledge, (evident in the many drawings of Leonardo da Vinci), which aided Salimbeni in his undertaking of the subject in this painting? (source: *A UFO in Pianello? By Isabella Dusi*
http://www.montalcino-tuscany.it/ufo_pianello.htm)

Saint Geremia's Contemplation - (1476-1478) Anon

On the pages of a richly illustrated 15th Century Bible - *the Urbinate Bible*, lies an unusual flying object. This superb manuscript, which is held in the Vatican library, was commissioned by Federico da Montefeltro, Duke of Urbino, at the studio of Vespasiano da Bisticci, (the renowned Florentine bookseller) who was the primary provider of manuscripts for the Urbino library.

The Bible is divided into two books: the Old and New Testament. The scribe of these volumes is considered to be Hugo de Cominellis or Hugues de Comminellis de Mazieres. The copy is a transcription of the canonic text of the Vulgate. The volumes are particularly important for the richness of their illustrations. Scholars have identified the hands of a number of different artists who cooperated in decorating these volumes, among them, panel painters, fresco painters and miniature painters. *The Urbinate Bible* is one of the rare examples of such artistic collaboration in Florence at the end of XV Century.[9]

The Urbinate's illustrators included Attavante, the Master of the Hamilton Xenophon, Francesco Rosselli, the brother of the most famous Cosimo, Francesco d'Antonio del Chierico and Domenico Ghirlandaio. Turning our attention to the UFO, it appears to resemble a fireball. Emanating from the flames surrounding the object we can see a perfectly

Figure 9) Saint Geremia's Contemplation (left):
© *Courtesy Vatican Library, Rome.*

straight yellow beam of light. Whether the object is the depiction of a natural phenomenon like a meteor or something more mysterious we will never know. However, we are left with a compelling image in a sacred book.

Title and Artist Unknown

This dramatic piece of artwork (figure 10 below) is from a wooden drawer held at the Earls D'Oltremond, Belgium. Moses is receiving the tablets containing the Ten Commandments. In the sky we can see several saucer-shaped objects.

The relevant section of the Bible reads :

"And it was as Moses came down from Mount Sinai and the two tablets of the testimony were in the hand of Moses when he came down from the mountain and Moses was not aware that the skin of his face was beaming when he spoke with Him." (Ex 34: 29).

Did Moses experience a close encounter with a UFO ?

You will notice he is depicted with horns. There are a number of artworks depicting Moses with horns including a statue by Michelangelo. The likeliest explanation for these appendages is that artists relied on Jerome's vulgate translation of the Old Testament. In this commonly available version, the 'rays of light' that were seen around Mose's face after his meet-

ing with God on Mt Sinai were mistranslated as 'horns'.

Figure 11 (right) is a still from a video showing a number of UFOs flying over the skies of Mexico in 1991. Perhaps the painting of Moses with the squadron of objects was an ancient depiction of what people see and film today.

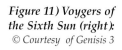

Figure 11) Voygers of the Sixth Sun (right):
© *Courtesy of Genisis 3*

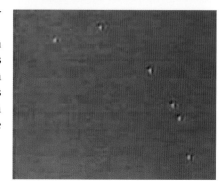

fortune ?

**Omme dit toß la vic à
eß breßue laquelle eß**

Figure 12) French Minature 1453 Le Livre Des Bonnes Moeurs (left):

This image is from a French book of 1453 titled Le Livre Des Bonnes Moeurs, by Jacques Legrand. It is held in Chantilly's Conde Museum. We find a medieval scene with what is quite clearly a golden patterned ball hovering in the centre of the image between the main characters. One bearded fellow in the background is acknowledging its presence by looking up and praying to it.

Conde Museum, Chantilly, France (ref 1338 ,297 part 15 B 8)

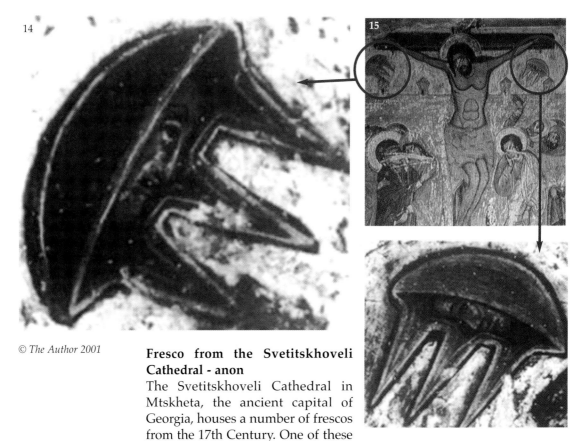

Fresco from the Svetitskhoveli Cathedral - anon

The Svetitskhoveli Cathedral in Mtskheta, the ancient capital of Georgia, houses a number of frescos from the 17th Century. One of these is shown above (figure 15). Two saucer shaped craft are depicted on either side of Christ on the cross. In the enlargements (above), you can see they contain faces. According to legend, the cathedral rose on the site of Georgia's first Christian church.[10] The outstanding Georgian architect Arsukisdze built the cathedral in 1010-1029. The cathedral was badly damaged at the end of the 14th Century during the invasion of Thameriane. The cupola was restored in the 15th Century. The facades are decorated with ornamental carvings and reliefs. Worthy of mention are the fragments of the surviving frescos including the one above.

Crucifixion and Resurrection of Christ - anon 1330

This fresco is located above the altar in the Visoki Decani Monastery in Kosovo, Yugoslavia. In the top left and top right of the image you can see two white flying objects. On closer examination, these objects contain figures in a sitting or crouched position (figure 14, right). Their hands seem to be placed as if

they are controlling the craft. These flying craft seem totally out if place in a 12th Century fresco. Who or whatever they represent is unclear, but it appears the artist has positioned them above the crucifixion scene as if to indicate they are heavenly beings observing the scene below.

According to historical records, the work on building the monastery lasted for eight years. It most likely started in 1327 and was completed during the time of King Stefan Dusan (1331-1355).

Baptism of Christ - **Aert De Gelder 1710 (see book cover)**

This Dutch painting catalogue number 633 can be found in the Fitzwilliam Museum, Cambridge, England. It was given to the museum by Lord Alwym Compton, Bishop of Ely in 1905. Apparently the previous owner, named Marianne, Countess of Alford, had bequeathed it to the donor in 1888. De Gelder was born in Dordrecht and spent all his life there; he was trained by Rembrandt and Samuel van Hoogstraten and

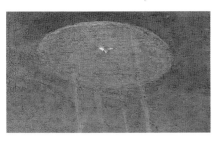 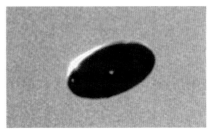

worked mostly with subjects from the *Old Testament* - the favourite subjects of his master and friend Rembrandt. He often used colours such as lilac and lemon yellow that were untypical of Rembrandt, and his palette was in general lighter. He had a fondness, just as Rembrandt did, for collecting objects and his studio was reminiscent of an old curiosity shop.[11] Looking at this painting, the observer can appreciate the artistic value of this work and the image of this huge, round disc hovering over John the Baptist and Jesus emitting brilliant, straight beams. It is quite compelling when looked at from a UFO perspective. Artistic historians tend to regard this UFO as simply an opening in the sky. When we examine the baptism scene in the Bible we read:

"And Jesus, when he was baptised, went straightaway out of the water; and, lo, the heavens were opened unto him and he saw the Spirit of God descending like

a dove, and lighting upon him." Matthew 3:16

Is De Gelder's UFO simply a hole in the heavens or could it be a craft of some kind? If we take on board the idea that ETs have been visiting us for thousands of years, we cannot rule out the idea that some artists were inspired by intelligences from elsewhere to include UFOs in their artworks. Could the Baptism of Christ have been a UFO event and De Gelder has unwittingly painted this scene?

To Almighty God - Anon 1882

Figure 18 (below):
Courtesy - Aleksander
Nevski Cathedral, Sofia,
Bulgaria
© http://www.discover-
bulgaria.com/insight.asp?
Article=true&PID=198

This fresco is from the vault of the Aleksander Nevski Cathedral in Sofia, Bulgaria. Notice the saucer-shaped object on the right hand side, above God's forefinger. The cathedral is one of Sofia's most famous monuments. This neo-Byzantine structure, which is surmounted by copper and golden domes, was built between 1882 and 1912 in honour of the Russian soldiers who died trying to liberate Bulgaria from Ottoman rule during the War of Liberation in 1878. The cathedral, which is also one of the finest buildings in the Balkan States, takes its name from Alexander Nevski, the patron saint of the family of the Russian Tsar at the time, Alexander II.

CHAPTER CONCLUSION

We have completed our journey through UFOs in western religious artwork. If these images of UFOs are not personal sightings reproduced on canvas or tapestry, could they originate from our collective unconscious just as Jung postulated? One scenario is that the artists observed UFOs and wanted to include them in their pictures for future generations. Hopefully, this book is fulfilling their wish and desire.

SOURCES

1) Web Gallery of Art *http://www.kfki.hu/~arthp/welcome.html*

2) *Notiziario UFO* n. 7 Luglio Agosto 1996 L'articolo di Daniele Bedini: *La Madonna del disco volante.*

3) Whitley Strieber's '*Hidden Agendas*' series UFO Briefing Document

4) Wundram, Manfred; *Paintings of the Renaissance*. 1997 Benedikt Taschen Verlag.

5) *European Painting* (in Russian). 1999. Moscow, Russia.

6) Walters, Ed and Frances; *The Gulf Breeze Sightings*. Bantam Press 1987

7) Ian Childers, *The Concise Oxford Dictionary of Art and Artists* (c) OUP 1900, 1996

8) Dr. Birgitt Borkopp Bayerisches National Museum.

9) *National Libraries Treasures of Europe*
:http://portico.bl.uk/gabriel/treasures/country/Vatican_City/vc01.html
Bibliography: *Miniature del Rinascimento*, catalogue of the exhibition, edited by L. Michelini Tocci, Vatican City, 1950, p. 82; M. Levi D'Ancona, *Miniatura e miniatori a Firenze dal XIV al XVI secolo*, Florence 1962 (*Storia della miniatura. Studi e documenti*, 1), pp. 68, 88, 108; Il Libro della Bibbia. *Esposizione di manoscritti e di edizioni a stampa della Biblioteca Apostolica Vaticana dal secolo III al secolo XVI*, edited by L. Michelini Tocci, Vatican City 1972, pp. 62-64; A. Garzelli, *La Bibbia di Federico da Montefeltro. Una officina libraria fiorentina*, 1476-1478, Rome 1977; *Raffaello e la Roma dei Papi*, [catalogue of the exhibition , Salone Sistino, gennaio-ottobre 1985, maggio-ottobre 1986] edited by G. Morello, Rome1986, p. 38; A.C. de la Mare, *Vespasiano da Bisticci e i copisti fiorentini di Federico*, in Federico di Montefeltro. *Lo stato, le arti, la cultura*, edited by G. Cerboni Baiardi, G. Chittolini, P. Floriani, Rome 1986 (Biblioteca del Cinquecento, 30), III, pp. 81-96; *I vangeli dei Popoli*. (edited by A.M. Piazzoni, G.Morello, F.D'Aiuto) Catalogue of the exhibition, Vatican City 2000.

10) Monuments of Ancient Georgia
http://www.rzuser.uni-heidelberg.de/~ci4/georgien/eklesiebi/mon2.htm

11) Fitzwilliam Museum, Cambridge. *http://www.fitzmuseum.cam.ac.uk/*
Olga's Gallery : *http://www.abcgallery.com/R/rembrandt/gelderbio.html*
Web Gallery of Art: *http://www.kfki.hu/~arthp/bio/g/gelder/biograph.html*

HISTORICAL UFO ACCOUNTS *Chapter Six*
498BC to 1900AD

"The face of heaven has been so often disfigured by bearded, hairy comets, torches, flames, columns, spears, shields, dragons, duplicate moons, suns and other things, that if one wanted to tell in an orderly fashion those that have happened since the birth of Jesus Christ only, and inquire about the causes of their origin, the lifetime of a single man would not be enough."
Pierre Boaistuau 1575.

This section lists in chronological order a selection of written accounts of UFO sightings from around the globe. Whilst a number could well relate to natural phenomena like comets or meteors, there are others that are more compelling. Some include landed objects; others include descriptions of mysterious beings. Some of these may point to an ET hypothesis. A rich source of ancient UFO accounts is to be found in the writings of Roman historians such as Pliny, Julius Obsequens, Livy and Cicero. The 4th Century historian Obsequens in fact catalogued 63 celestial happenings in his book *Liber Prodigiorum*.

498 BC *"... Castor and Pollux were seen fighting in our army on horseback... Nor do we forget that when the Locrians defeated the people of Crotona in a battle on the banks of the river Sagra, it was known the same day at the Olympian Games. The voices of the Fauns have been heard and deities have appeared in forms so visible that they have compelled everyone who is not senseless or hardened to impiety to confess the presence of the Gods."* [1]

325 BC *"There in the stillness of the night both consuls are said to have been visited by the same apparition, a man of greater than human stature, and more majestic, who declared that the commander of one side and the army of the other must be offered up to the Manes and to Mother Earth."* [2]

223 BC *"At Ariminium a bright light like the day blazed out at night; in many portions of Italy three moons became visible in the night time."* [3]

222 BC *"Also three moons have appeared at once, for instance, in the consulship of Gnaeus Domitius and Gaius Fannius."* [4]

218 BC *"In Amiterno district in many places were seen the appearance of men*

The illustrations on the opposite page are from (top) a 18th Century woodcut of an aerial vision as seen by two night watchmen. (bottom) A 13th Century French manuscript, which depicts a nobleman riding a horse and pointing directly at a disc-shaped object. (see page 106-107)

103

in white garments from far away. The orb of the sun grew smaller. At Praeneste glowing lamps from heaven. At Arpi a shield in the sky. The moon contended with the sun and during the night two moons were seen. Phantom ships appeared in the sky." [5]

217 BC *"At Faleri the sky had seemed to be rent as it were with a neat fissure and through the opening a bright light had shone."*[6]

216 BC In Rome, in Boaria Square, an ox spontaneously rose to the third floor of a house and then, frightened by the people shouting, the ox felt down on the ground. Images of ships were seen in the sky and the Temple of the Hope was hit by lightning. This happened during the consulate of Gneo Servilio Gemino and in the second consulate of Gaio Quinzio Flaminio (215 BC and 217 BC - 535 years since Rome foundation). We can see a depiction of these incidents in the illustration (right). [7]

214 BC *"At Hadria an altar was seen in the sky and about it the forms of men in white clothes."*[8]

170 BC *"At Lanupium, a remarkable spectacle of a fleet of ships was seen in the air."* Conrad Wolfhart, Lycothenes (1518-1567), a Swiss philosopher, theologian and professor of grammar, whose actual surname was Wolfhart. He chronicled inexplicable phenomena in his compendium *Prodigiorum Ac Ostentorum Chronicon*, published in 1567.

163 BC *"In the consulship of Tiberius Gracchus and Manius Juventus at Capua the sun was seen by night. At Formice two suns were seen by day. The sky was afire. In Cephallenia a trumpet seemed to sound from the sky. There was a rain of earth. A windstorm demolished houses and laid crops flat in the field. By night an apparent sun shone at Pisaurum."* [9]

122 BC *"In Gaul three suns and three moons were seen."* [10]

99 BC During the consulate of Gaio Mario and Lucio Valerio, a meteor had been seen over Tarquinia (a town near Rome). Additionally, at around sunset a round body similar to a shield was seen flying from west to east. These two sightings are depicted right; you can see witnesses on the ground pointing up to the sky. [11]

90 BC Spoletium, Rome. *"At Aernarie, while Livius Troso was promulgating the laws at the beginning of the Italian war, at sunrise, there came a terrific noise in the sky, and a globe of fire appeared burning in the north. In*

the territory of Spoletium, a globe of fire, of golden color, fell to the earth gyrating. It then seemed to increase in size, rose from the earth and ascended into the sky, where it obscured the sun with its brilliance. It revolved toward the eastern quadrant of the sky." [12]

85 BC *"In the consulship of Lucius Valerius and Caius Marius, a burning shield scattering sparks ran across the sky."* [13]

81 BC *"Near Spoletium a gold-colored fireball rolled down to the ground, increased in size; seemed to move off the ground toward the east and was big enough to blot out the sun."* [14]

72 BC *"But one being came in sight of his enemies, he was astonished at their numbers, and thought to forbear fighting, and wear out time. But Marius, whom Serto-rius had sent out of Spain to Mithridates with forces under him, stepping out and challenging him, he prepared for battle. In the very instant before joining battle, without any perceptible alteration preceding, all of a sudden the sky opened, and a large luminous body fell down in the midst between the armies, in shape like a hogshead, but in colour like melted silver, insomuch that both armies in alarm withdrew. This wonderful prodigy happened in Phrygia, near Otryae."* [15]

66 BC *"In the consulship of Gnaeus Octavius and Gaius Suetonius a spark was seen to fall from a star and increase in size as it approached the earth. After becoming as large as the moon it diffused a sort of cloudy daylight and then returning to the sky changed into a torch. This is the only record of its occurrence. It was seen by the proconsul Silenus and his suite. "* [16]

48 BC *"Thunderbolts had fallen upon Pompey's camp. A fire had appeared in the air over Caesar's camp and had fallen upon Pompey's ... In Syria two young men announced the result of the battle (in Thessaly) and vanished."* [17]

42 BC *"In Rome light shone so brightly at nightfall that people got up to begin work as though day had dawned. At Murtino three suns were seen about the third hour of the day, which presently drew together in a single orb."* [18]

70 AD *"On the 21st of May a demonic phantom of incredible size... for before sunset there appeared in the air over the whole country chariots and armed troops coursing the clouds and surrounding cities."* [19]

80 AD *"When the Roman emperor, Agricola was in Scotland, wondrous flames were seen in the skies over Caledon Wood, all one winter night. Everywhere the air burned, and on many nights, when the weather was serene, a ship was seen in the air moving fast."* [20]

98 AD *"At sunset, a burning shield passed over the sky at Rome. It came sparkling from the west and passed over to the east."* [21]

329 AD Alexander the Great had two UFO encounters that were recorded. During his invasion of Asia in 329, while crossing a river, Alexander and his men saw what was described as gleaming, silver shields in the sky. The objects repeatedly swooped down at the soldiers, scattering men and horses and creating quite a panic. Seven years later, while attacking Venice in the eastern Mediterranean, observers on both sides of the conflict reported another incredible event. Objects appeared in the sky. One of the objects suddenly shot a beam of light at the city wall, crumbling it to dust. This allowed Alexander's troops to easily take the city. (Alexander mentions this in his letters to Aristotle.)

356 AD Golgotha, Israel. A magnificent ethereal cross appeared over the sky. It was two miles in diameter and spanned as far as the Mount of Olives. It was witnessed by the entire city. It continued to float over the city for several hours. The light was described as brighter than the sun. The sighting occurred immediately following the inauguration of Saint Cyril as bishop. (This sighting is mentioned in his letters to Emperor Constantine.) [22]

494 AD These two images are from Lycothene's *Prodigiorum Ac Ostentorum Chronicon*. The text states that two UFOs were sighted in the year 494 in an area we now know as Milan during a battle between the Swiss and the Italians and was documented in a manuscript known as *Annales Basilea*.

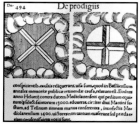

673 - 738 AD Bede, an Anglo Saxon theologian, historian and chronologist mentions several references to beams of light which stretched between the sky and human corpses. On one occasion, a light from heaven played over the body of a drowned abbot for several nights. [23]

776 AD Sigiburg Castle, France. A translation of *Annales Laurissenses* (books about historical and religious events) reads:
"Now when the Saxons perceived things were not going in their favour, they began to erect scaffolding from which they could bravely storm the castle itself. But God is good as well as just. He overcame their valour, and on the same day they prepared an assault against the Christians, who lived within the castle, the glory of God appeared in manifestation above the church within the fortress. Those watching outside in that place, of whom many still live to this very day, say they beheld the likeness of two large shields reddish in colour in motion above the church ..." [24]

The two images on the opposite page and on page 106, date from a 13th Century manuscript. The first picture depicts a French soldier with his arms up, an object is above him in the sky. It is shaped like a sphere with little portholes around it's rim. The artist is trying to convey the movement of the object by drawing flame-like shapes from it. The second image depicts a nobleman riding a horse and pointing directly at a disc-shaped object. Again the object has porthole like circles around it. Imagine back then what the witnesses must have thought on viewing two UFOs. Today a witness would think it was a secret military aircraft or an extraterrestrial device. Back then, it was assumed knights piloted the discs. On reflection we are left wandering whether the UFOs appearance was by accident, or whether whoever was behind the objects had the intention to influence the course of events on that day.

800 AD France. In the writings of Agobard, Archbishop of Lyons, is the strange tale of three men and a woman who were seen alighting from an aerial ship during the Ninth Century. An angry mob gathered around the four strangers. Their emperor, Charlemagne, had issued edicts that imposed penalties on aerial travellers. These four visitors were thought to be magicians sent by Charlemagne's enemy, Grimaldus, Duke of Beneventum, to destroy the French harvests. In vain, the four strangers protested that they were compatriots and had been carried off by miraculous men who had shown them unheard of marvels. As the people were about to throw their captors into the fire, Agobard, their well-respected Archbishop, interrupted them. He pronounced both stories to be untrue. He declared that since it was impossible for people to fall out of the sky, it could not have happened. The citizens of Lyons, respecting the authority of their Archbishop, rejected the evidence witnessed by their own eyes and liberated the four strangers.[25]

919 AD An object like a flaming torch was seen in the sky, together with spheres, which flew over Hungary giving out a brighter light than the stars.[26]

989 AD Japan. On the 3rd August during a period of great social unrest, three round objects of unusual brilliance were observed; later they joined together.[26]

1034 A rare typeset book, now preserved in a museum at Verdun, France. Hartmann Schedel, author of the book *Liber Chronicarum*, describes a strange fiery sphere - seen in 1034 - soaring through the sky in a straight course from south to east and then veering toward the setting sun. The illustration accompanying the account shows a cigar-shaped form haloed by flames, sailing through a blue sky over a green, rolling countryside.[28]

1060 Jiangsu, China. The Mandarin astronomer Shen Kuo, described with the scientific terminology of those times a circular object, *"bright as a pearl"* emitting a strong light during the day and projecting a different shadow than that of the Sun, on a surface of about 5 square kilometers. On each appearance, the dogs of the area started to bark in a wild way. The UFO came back frequently to fly over the same village for ten years.[29]

27th October 1180 A term equivalent to our flying saucer was actually used by the Japanese approximately 700 years before it came into use in the West. Ancient documents describe an unusual shining object seen the night of October 27, 1180, as a flying earthenware vessel. After a while the object, which had been heading northeast from a mountain in Kii Province, changed its direction and vanished below the horizon, leaving a luminous trail.[30]

24th September 1235 What might be called the first official investigation of a UFO sighting, occurred in Japan in 1235. During the night of September 24, while General Yoritsume and his army were encamped, they observed mysterious lights in the heavens. The lights were seen in the southwest for many hours, winging, circling and moving in loops. The general ordered a full-scale scientific investigation of these strange events. The report finally submitted to him has the soothing ring of many contemporary explanations offered for UFO phenomena. In essence it read: the whole thing is completely natural, *"General, It is only the wind making the stars sway."* [31]

September 1271 The famous priest, Nichiren, was about to be beheaded at Tatsunokuchi, Kamakura, when there appeared in the sky an object like a full moon, shiny and bright. Needless to say, the officials panicked and the execution was not carried out.[32]

1361 A flying object described as being shaped like a drum, about twenty feet in diameter emerged from the inland sea off western Japan.[33]

1394 England. In the winter of 1394 a wheel- or barrel-shaped object appeared in several areas of England:
"A certain thing appeared in the likeness of fire in many parts of... England... every night. This fiery apparition, oftentimes when anybody went alone, it would go with him, and would stand still when he stood still... To some it appeared in the likeness of a turning wheel burning; to othersome round in the likeness of a barrel, flashing out flames of fire at the head; to others in the likeness of a long burning lance."[34]

1453 Constantinople. *"A fire descended from the sky, stood over the City, and enveloped her with light all night long"*. Written during the Turkish siege of Constantinople.

1458 On the 2nd January 1458, Japan, a bright object resembling the full moon was seen in the sky, and this apparition was followed by 'curious signs' in heaven and Earth. Two months later five stars appeared, circling the moon. They changed colour three times and vanished suddenly.[35]

1st November 1461 A fiery thing like an iron rod of good length and as large as one half of the moon was seen in the sky, over Arras, France for less than a quarter of an hour. This object was also described as being *"shaped like a ship from which fire was seen flowing."*[36]

February 1465 Italy. The illustration is from *Notabilia Temporum* by Angelo de Tummulillis. It describes a flaming girder seen in the sky during the reign of Enrico IV.

9th March 1468 Japan. A dark object, which made a *"sound like a wheel"*, flew from Mt. Kasuga towards the west at midnight.[37]

1479 Arabia. An object was sighted looking like a sharply pointed wooden beam. An artist's concept, based on eyewitness testimony is shown on the next page. (This illustration is taken from a book entitled *Prodigiorum Ac Ostentorum Chronicon* by Conrad Lycothenes). Compare the 15th Century illustration with this object adjacent to it, photographed by Caroll Watts near Wellington, Texas on 11th June 1967. Watts estimated the craft to be 100 ft in length. I have also seen a similar object painted by the Nineteenth Century French artist Paul Sérusier.

8th November 1517 *"A great blue sign shining like a face of a man"* appeared in the western sky over Moldavia. It remained quite a long time, at the same place, after which it 'hid itself' in the sky again."*[38]

© Conrad Lycothenes

© Caroll Watts

14th April 1561 The image on the right is of an actual sighting that occurred in Nuremberg on the 14th April, 1561. It appeared in a local broadsheet and was a woodcut by Hans Glasser. The globes, crosses and tubes began to fight one another, and this went on for an hour. Then they all fell to Earth, as if on fire, and faded slowly away producing a lot of steam. Afterwards, a

black spear-like object was seen, and the whole event was taken to be a divine warning. © The Wickiana Collection, Zurich Central Library.

1563 Bergen, Norway. A priest, Absalon Pederssøn Beyer, together with Christern Ulff and a goldsmith, their wives and their servants, observed a round, unnatural 'black cloud' passing in front of the moon and covering it. A blaze of smoke and fire was then emitted by the black 'cloud', and they all heard a whistling sound. The 'cloud' then moved back and forth, then disappeared. This lasted from half past 7 until 9 o'clock.[39]

1566 This broadsheet picture (left) by Samuel Coccius illustrates a UFO sighting over Basel, Switzerland in 1566. 'Large black globes' appeared in the skies. Meteors or something extraterrestrial? It is held at the Wickiana Collection, Zurich Central Library.

5th December 1577   Tubingen, Germany. Objects came out of the clouds resembling large, tall and wide hats and they landed in great numbers and in a variety of colours. (This quote comes from Pierre Boaistuau's 1594 book, *Chronicling Strange Happenings*. He reports that sightings of entities also accompanied this event, but goes into no detail.)

1580 Pedro Sarmiento, a navigator approaching the Strait of Magellen stated *"we saw a round and flat thing appear, red like fire, shaped like a shield, that rose up on the air or on the wind. It became longer as it went over a mountain and, in the form of a lance high above the mount, it's shape became like a half-moon between red and white in colour."* [40]

May 1606. Kyoto, Japan. A whirling ball of fire resembling a red wheel hovered near Nijo Castle and was observed by many samurai. [41]

This is a reconstruction of the '3 carriages' being fired upon by the startled inhabitants as illustrated by the French UFO group G.E.O.S. (Group d'Etudes des Objects Spatiaux) some years ago.

© Group d'Etudes des Objects Spatiaux

August 1608 Nice and Genoa. An ancient document in the Municipal Archives of Nice, France describes a frightening encounter, informing us of strange events that happened in this town and in Genoa, Italy, in the August of 1608. This translation was provided to the author by Natalie Broulliette:

FRIGHTENING SPEECHES OF THE SIGNS, WHICH APPEARED ON THE SEA OF GENOA AT THE BEGINNING OF LAST AUGUST OF THE YEAR 1608.

"At the beginning of the month of August of the year 1608 on the sea of Genoa were seen the most horrible sights that in man's memory was talked about or written about. Some had human form with arms seemingly covered with scales and had in each of their 2 hands 2 horrible flying snakes which wrapped around their arms and only appeared from the belly button up out of the sea and were producing some so horrible cries that it was the most frightening thing and sometimes they dived in the sea and then came out in other places far from there shouting cries so frightening that many were ill with the fear they had. They saw some that resembled female bodies; others had bodies like human bodies all covered with scales but with a head in the shape of dragons."

"Since the 1st day of that month they have been ordinarily seen at the great astonishment of all the people of Genoa. The "lordship" provided some canons in an attempt to make them shift out of this place and some 800-canon shots were but in vain, as they were in no way astonished. The Churches united and going for the real remedy made processions and ordered fasting. The good fathers "Capucins" ordered the 40 hours fasting to try and appease the anger of their God with their salutation remedies."

"On the 15th August near the port of Genoa three carriages each pulled by six creatures of fire resembling dragons. And walked the said carriages one beside the other and were pulled by the said signs which had their snakes and were all producing frightening screams and were getting nearer Genoa so that the spectators at least the majority aston-

ished fled, fearing the effect of such a miracle, but, as they did ... three times the long bridge so powerful in noise that they made the surrounding mountains echo, they were all lost in the sea and since then no one has seen or heard any news from them. This brought a great shame to many of the citizens of Genoa, some died out of fear like among others, the son of the Lord Gasparino of Loro and also the brother of Lord Anthonio Bagatelo, many women also were afflicted and had such fears that they died."[42]

15th August 1663 As the people of the village Robozero (in the Bolozero district, Russia) were in church, they heard a loud noise in the sky and many people left the church to see what was happening. One of them, farmer Levka Pedorov, described events to the monastery monk, who documented them in script. At midday a *"great ball of fire"* descended from the south in a clear blue sky over Robozero and moved across the church to a nearby lake. The 'ball' was 45 metres in diameter and two beams of 'fire' were shooting out from the front. It then proceeded to move from the south to the west (500 metres from Pedorov) and disappeared, only to reappear an hour later over the same lake. It remained there for an hour and a half. Fishermen in a boat on the lake a mile away from Pedorov said the light from the 'ball', which lit up the nine metre deep lake, burned them. Fish were seen jumping onto the banks. Pedorov described the water as being *"covered with rust under the glow..."* Another case, similar in many ways, is said to have occurred on November 30 in 1663, also over Robozero, but there are only brief documents relating to it in, *St. Petersburgs Historical Files* by the archeological commission part IV in 1842, where the monk's document is also held.

16th August 1670 An illustration (above) of a UFO sighting over Touraine, France.[43]

1680 A French coin or medal, commemorates the sighting of a wheel-like object in the same year (right).

4th November 1697 The drawing on the next page shows a UFO sighting over Hamburg, Germany. The objects were described as 'two glowing wheels'.

5th February 1709. Location not men-

tioned. *"Here was a great sign in the sky on 5th February a Wednesday. Two large columns of fire were revealed, one in the east, the other on the west, and as they moved they formed the letter 'A'. They united after this and turned into a rainbow, emitting strong light for three hours, before their disappearance."*[44]

London, 1710. An aerial vision seen by two night watchmen. This woodcut (below) shows the 18th century equivalent of a UFO sighting by a police patrol.
© Mary Evans Picture Library

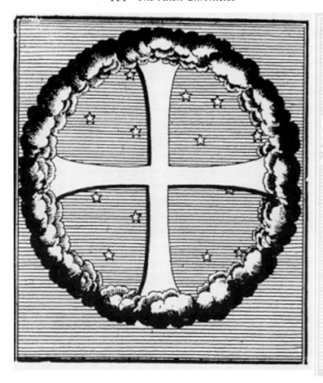

20th August/8th Sept 1718. Sciantun, China. These two UFOs (symbols left and tinted behind text on this page) were seen over Chinese skies. [45]

8th December 1733 James Cracker of Fleet, a small town in Dorset, England, saw a silvery disc fly overhead in broad daylight.

"I saw something in the sky which appeared in the north but vanished from my sight, as it was intercepted by trees, from my vision. I was standing in a valley. The weather was warm, the sun shone brightly. On a sudden it re-appeared, darting in and out of my sight with an amazing coruscation. The colour of this phenomenon was like burnished, or new-washed silver. It shot with speed like a star falling in the night. But it had a body much larger and a train longer than any shooting star I have seen."

"Next day Mr. Edgecombe informed me that he and another gentleman had seen this strange phenomenon at the same time as I had. It was about 15 miles from where I saw it, and steering a course from east to north." [46]

6th December 1737 In the afternoon, a large 'symbol' appeared in the western sky *"red as blood and very broad"* over Bucharest, Romania. After remaining in the sky for two hours, it split up into two parts but later became united once again in the western sky as before. [47]

16th December 1742 This is a scan from vol. 42 of the *Philosophical Transactions* 1742 describing a sighting of a UFO. Alongside is a contemporary reconstruction (top of the opposite page) depicting the object described:

A seemed to be a light Flame, turning backwards from the Refistance the Air made to it. *B B* a bright Fire like burning Charcoal, inclofed as it were in an open Cafe, of which the Frame *C C C* was quite opaque, like Bands of Iron. At *D* iffued forth a Train or Tail of light Flame, more bright at *D*, and growing gradually fainter at *E, f*, as to be tranfparent more than half its Length. The Head feemed about half a Degree in Diameter, the Tail near 3 Degrees in Length, and about one Eighth of a Degree in Thickness.
C. M.

"As I was returning home from the Royal Society to Westminster, on Thursday Dec 16 1742, 8.40 PM being about the middle of the Parade in St James Park I saw a light arrive from behind the trees and houses in the south by west point, which I took at first for a large sky rocket; but when it had risen to the height of about 20 Degrees, it took motion nearly parallel to the horizon, but waved in this manner, and went on to the north by east point over the houses. It seemed to be very near that I thought it passed over Queens Square, the island in the park, the canal, and I lost sight of it over the Haymarket. Its motion was so very low, that I had it above half a minute in view, and therefore had time to contemplate its appearance fully, which was what is seen in the annexed figure."

January 2 1749 Japan. Three objects shaped like the moon appeared and were observed for four days. This sighting caused much social unrest and later people observed two 'suns'.[48]

September 1768 The famous writer Goethe had a UFO sighting whilst travelling from Frankfurt to the University of Leipzig. He described seeing *"a sort of amphitheatre"*, wonderfully illuminated with many little lights, jumping about dazzling his eyes. Goethe mentions this in the sixth book of his autobiography.
[49]

18th August 1783 This illustration depicts a sighting that occurred at 9.45pm on the evening of 18th August 1783, when four witnesses on the terrace of Windsor Castle observed a luminous object in the skies of the Home Counties of England. The sighting was recorded the following year in the *Philosophical Transactions of the Royal Society*. According to this report, witnesses observed an oblong cloud moving more or less parallel to the  horizon. The image was captured by Thomas Sandby (a founder of the Royal Academy) and his brother Paul, both of whom witnessed the event.

16th November 1793 Bucharest, Romania. A witness said, as he was dining with a friend named Constandin Poenaru, in Floresti, that on the previous day: *"the moon carried out a miracle - she made a journey along the sky for half an hour"*.[50]

17th December 1799 Migne, Poitiers, France. Three thousand people witnessed a magnificent luminous object shining brighter than the sun and clearly 'not of this world'. It was described as shaped like a cross, with the length being 40ft and the cross member 4 feet. Mgr. De Bouille published an account of this apparition and later received two briefs from Pope Leo XII.

1803 This illustration (on page 114) is from a book *Ume No Chiri (Dust of Apricot)* published in 1803. A foreign ship and crew witnessed this strange object at Haratonohama (Haratono Seashore) in Hitachi no Kuni (Ibaragi Prefecture),

Japan. According to the explanation in the drawing, the outer shell was made of iron and glass, and strange letters shown in this drawing were seen inside the ship.

1812 Bucovina, Romania.

"Towards noon a large star with many rays appeared and in the night she ascended higher and flew in the direction of the Russians; afterwards she returned and went to the west, where the beams where extinguished. Thus did the star reveal herself for four months." It was during the war between the Russians, French and Germans. Witness: Stan Irinie from Sâcele-Brasov.[51]

1836 In the town of Szeged, Hungary, near the Romanian border, spherical lights and the appearance of what looked like a 'lady in white' created uproar in a part of the town.[52]

29/30th August 1837 Romania. On September 2nd (the sighting occurred on 29/30th of August), the paper *Albina Românesca* wrote: *"In the course of this night a meteor was seen, or a physical phenomenon (over Tîrgu-Neamt and Dorohoi. ed.note). It was a sphere, lit up, about 12 hands long and broad (about 3 metres). It descended in the twilight and the whole field shone with a powerful light and glow."*

1842 Orenburg, Russia. Small metal objects, perfectly hexagonal, fell out of the sky after a 'strange cloud' was seen hanging over the town of Orenburg for a considerable time.[53]

1843 In March that year a UFO-flap was building up over Europe. Some say that it was a comet, as the phenomenon came back during several nights, grew larger in scale and appeared and disappeared at the same place. But on March 9th it was accompanied by an object the shape of a 'fire-ball', which vanished after a few seconds in the form of a lightning. As the object appeared on the west-side (Europe), it was described as pyramidal and the side towards the horizon was shorter and not so strongly lit up; the other side was broader.[54]

August 1863 Madrid, Spain.
"The night before last there was observed on the horizon a luminous body that appeared towards the east, and it was promptly thought to be a comet. It was of a reddish colour, and on the top there could be seen an appendix or crown, that was doubtlessly ablaze. It was stationary for a long time (mantúvose mucho tiempo); but later it began to move quickly in different directions: horizontally, rising and lowering."[55]

19th October 1865 Missouri, USA. An account from a newspaper *Missouri*

Democrat of a possible UFO crash:

"A STRANGE STORY-REMARKABLE DISCOVERY-Mr. James Lumley, an old Rocky Mountain trapper, who has been stopping at the Everett House for several days, makes a most remarkable statement to us, and one which, if authenticated, will produce the greatest excitement in the scientific world.

Mr. Lumley states that about the middle of last September, he was engaged in trapping in the mountains about seventy-five or one hundred miles above the Great Falls of the Upper Missouri, and in the neighborhood of what is known as Cadotte Pass. Just after sunset one evening, he beheld a bright luminous body in the heavens, which moved with great rapidity in an easterly direction. It was plainly visible for at least five seconds, when it suddenly separated into particles, resembling, as Mr. Lumley describes it, the bursting of a sky-rocket in the air. A few minutes later, he heard a heavy explosion, which jarred the earth very perceptibly, and this was shortly after followed by a rushing sound, like a tornado sweeping through the forest. A strong wind sprang up about the same time, but suddenly subsided. The air was also filled with a peculiar odor of a sulphurous character.

These incidents would have made a slight impression on the mind of Mr. Lumley, but for the fact that on the ensuing day he discovered, at the distance of about two miles from his camping place, that, as far as he could see in either direction a path had been cut through the forest, several road wide, giant trees uprooted or broken off near the ground- the tops of hills shaved off and the earth plowed up in many places. Great and widespread havoc was everywhere visible.

Following up this track of desolation, he soon ascertained the cause of it in the shape of an immense stone driven into the side of a mountain. An examination of this stone, or so much of it as was visible, showed that it was divided into compartments that in various places it was carved with curious hieroglyphics. More than this, Mr. Lumley also discovered fragments of a substance resembling glass, and here and there dark stains, as though caused by a liquid. He is confident that the hieroglyphics are the work of human hands, and that the stone itself, although but a fragment of an immense body, must have been used for some purpose by animated beings. Strange as this story appears, Mr. Lumley relates it with so much sincerity that we are forced to accept it as true. It is evident that the stone which he discovered, was a fragment of the meteor which was visible in this section in September last. It will be remembered that it was seen in Leavenworth, Galena and in this city by Col. Bonneville. At Leavenworth it was seen to separate into particles or explode.
Astronomers have long held that it is probable that the heavenly bodies are inhabited — even the comets — and it may be that the meteors are also. Possibly, meteors could be used as a means of conveyance by the inhabitants of other planets, in exploring space, and it may be that hereafter some future Columbus, from Mercury or Uranus, may land on this planet by means of a meteoric conveyance, and take full possession thereof — as did the Spanish navigators of the New World in 1492, and eventually drive what is known as the "human race" into a condition of the most abject servitude. It has always been a favorite theory with many that there must be a race superior to us, and this may

at some future time be demonstrated in the manner we have indicated."

25th July 1868 Parramatta, NSW, Australia. A surveyor experienced a vision involving heads floating by him and subsequently observed an 'ark' moving along the same path and landing in Parramatta Park, Sydney. A voice spoke to him and asked if he wished to enter the ark. He replied that he would and was 'floated' to the object. A 'spirit' appeared like a *"neutral tint shade and the shape of a man in his usual frock dress."* He was shown around the ark, after which the spirit disappeared. The man awoke next morning, *"deeply impressed with the vision of the night."*[56]

July 1868 Copiapo, Chile. A strange 'aerial construction' bearing lights and making engine noises, flew low over this town. Local people also described it as a 'giant bird' covered with large scales producing a metallic noise. Although not an actual landing, this is the first instance of close observation of an unknown object at low altitude in the Nineteenth Century.[57]

7th December 1872 Banbury, Great Britain. At King's Sutton an object resembling a haystack flew on an irregular course. Sometimes high, sometimes very low it was accompanied by fire and dense smoke. It produced the same effect as a tornado, felling trees and walls. It suddenly vanished.[58]

1873 South Australia. A bright light followed a sailing ship for almost an hour. Captain Lebman of the ship *Adelheid*, described the light as 'milky - white'. He said, *"It came over the ship in waves, with one wave every two seconds between 10.30pm and 11.30pm at night. A shuddering feeling was experienced at the sight."* He went on to say, *"...and the intense light made the eyes ache. During the whole time the sea was illuminated, though not vividly. For a quarter of an hour after it was over flashes of light were perceptible in the water."* [59]

1874 A Professor Schafarick sees: *"a strange, brightly lit object which passed slowly across the moon and remained visible for some time afterwards. I do not know what to make of it..."*[60]

15th May 1879 Persian Gulf. Two very large 'wheels' were seen spinning in the air and slowly coming to the surface of the sea. Estimated diameter: 40 metres. Distance between the objects: 150m. Speed: 80km/h/ Duration: 35 min. Witnesses aboard the ship *Vulture*.[61]

1880 Aldershot, Great Britain. A strange being dressed in tight-fitting clothes and shining helmet soared over the heads of two sentries, who fired without result. The apparition stunned them with something described as 'blue fire'.[62]

1880 Eastern Venezuela. A 14-year-old boy saw a luminous ball descending from the sky and hovering near him. He felt somehow 'drawn' to it, but succeeded in backing away in spite of his terror.[63]

26th March 1880 Lamy, New Mexico. Four men walking near Galisteo Junction were surprised as they heard voices coming from a 'strange balloon', which flew over them. It was shaped like a fish and seemed to be guided by a large fanlike device. There were eight to ten figures aboard. Their language was not understood. The object flew low over Galisteo Junction and rose rapidly towards the east.[64]

30th July 1880 Witnesses in St. Petersburg saw a large spherical light accompanied by two smaller stars or spheres, follow the course of a ravine for three minutes, after which they suddenly vanished.[65]

11th June 1881 Between Melbourne and Sydney (at sea), Australia. The two sons of the Prince of Wales, one of them the future king of England, were cruising aboard *La Bacchante* when an object resembling a fully lighted ship was seen (*"a phantom vessel all aglow"*).[66]

2nd November, 1885 Scutari (Turkey). A luminous object circled the harbour at an altitude of around 5-6 metres, illuminating the whole town with a blueish green flame. It made several circles above the ferry boat pier (for one and half minutes), before plunging into the sea.[67]

12th November, 1887 Cape Race, Atlantic Ocean. A huge sphere of fire was observed rising out of the ocean by witnesses aboard the *Siberian*. It rose to an altitude of 16 metres, flew against the wind and came close to the ship. Then 'dashed off' toward the southeast. Duration: 5 min.[68]

February 1893 North China Sea. The ship, *H.M.S. Carolina*, was sailing in the North China Sea, when a report from an officer of unusual light activity in the sky came to the attention of Captain J.N. Norcross. The officer told Captain Norcross that the lights appeared sometimes in a huge mass, others spread out in unusual patterns. He said that they resembled Chinese lanterns set between the masts of a ship. The next night, these strange lights reappeared, but with a reddish glow and emanating small amounts of smoke.

1893 Central New South Wales, Australia. A farmer claimed that a saucer-shaped object landed in one of his paddocks. As the farmer approached the object, a man in strange clothing emerged from it. The farmer walked towards the man, who shone some kind of 'torch' at him throwing him to the ground and stunning him. When he came to, the man and the object had gone. The hand where the 'torch beam' had hit him was paralyzed for life.[69]

30th August 1895 At about 8pm, England. An account by the distinguished lexicographer and philologist, James Augustus Henry Murray, of an object he observed while walking across the Oxford University campus.
"I saw a brilliant luminous body which suddenly emerged over the tops of the trees before me on the left and moved eastward across the sky above and in front of me. It's appearance was, at first glance, such as to suggest a brilliant meteor, considerably larger than

Venus at her greatest brilliancy, but the slowness of the motion...made one doubt whether it was not some artificial firework....I watched....as it continued its course toward the eastern horizon. It did not explode, emit any spark, or leave any train or track; but it became rapidly dimmer...and finally disappeared behind a tree....The fact that it so perceptibly grew fainter as it receded seems to imply that it had not a very great elevation....[Its] course was slower than any meteor I have ever seen."

1896 Arolla, near Zermatt, Swiss Alps. Author, Aleister Crowley, was walking in the mountains when he suddenly saw two little men. He made a gesture to them, but they did not seem to pay attention and disappeared among the rocks.[70]

If the records are to be believed, there were nearly a hundred sightings of UFOs or 'airships' as they were called in the United States in 1896-1897, most of them in the mid-west.

26th November 1896 California, USA.
"When [the mysterious light] first appeared it was seen moving rapidly from the north-east and heading in a southwesterly direction. As it neared the southern boundary of the city [of Sacramento] it turned directly toward the west and after passing the city went south, being distinctly visible for upward of 20 minutes." Many prominent individuals including Deputy Secretary of State George A. McCalvy, District Attorney Frank D. Ryan, and E. D. McCabe, the governor's personal secretary, observed this light.[71]

26th March 1897 Sioux City, Iowa. Approximate date. An anchor dropped from an unknown flying machine 22 km north of the town caught Robert Hibbard. He was dragged over 10 m and fell as his clothes were torn.[72]

28th March 1897 Omaha, Nebraska. The majority of the population observed an object arriving from the southeast. It looked like a huge light, flew north-westward and slowly came to a low altitude. A crowd gathered at a street corner to watch it.[73]

1st April 1897 Everest, Kansas. The whole town saw an object fly under the cloud ceiling. It came down slowly, then flew away very fast to the southeast. When directly over the town, it swept the ground with its powerful light. It was seen to rise up at fantastic speed until barely discernible, then to come down again and sweep low over the witnesses. At one point it remained stationary for 5 minutes at the edge of a low cloud, which it illuminated. All could clearly see the silhouette of the craft.[74]

12th April 1897 Nilwood, Illinois. On the property of Z. Thacker, 19 km north of Carlinville, an unknown object landed. Before the three witnesses could reach it, the craft, which was shaped like a cigar with a dome, rose slowly and left majestically toward the north. Witnesses: Edward Teeples, William Street and Franklin Metcalf.[75]

12th April 1897 Girard, near Green Ridge, Illinois. A large crowd of 1800 miners saw an unknown object land 3 kilometres north of Green Ridge and 4 km south of Girard. The night operator of the Chicago-and-Alton Railroad, Paul McCramer, stated that he came sufficiently close to the craft to see a man emerge from it to repair the machinery. Traces were found over a large area. The object itself was elongated like a ship with a roof and a double canopy. It left towards the north.[76]

14th April 1897 Gas City, Indiana. An object landed 2 km south of Gas City on the property of John Roush, terrifying the farmers and causing the horses and cattle to stampede. Six occupants of the ship came out and seemed to make some repairs. Before the crowd could approach the object, it rose rapidly and flew toward the east.[77]

14th April 1897 Cleveland, Ohio. Joseph Singler, captain of the *Sea Wing*, was fishing with S. H. Davis, of Detroit, when they saw on the lake what they thought was a ship, about 13 m long, with a canopy. A man, about 25 years old, wearing a hunting jacket and a cap, was fishing from the deck of the object. Near him were a woman and a 10-year old child. When the *Sea Wing* came close to the craft, a large, coloured balloon rose from the object, which flew up with it to an altitude of about 150 m and circled 'like a hawk' before flying away.[78]

15th April 1897 Linn Grove, Iowa. A large object was seen to fly in the morning slowly toward the north. It seemed ready to land and five men (F. G. Ellis, James Evans, David Evans, Joe Croaskey, Benjamin Buland) drove towards it. About 7 km north of Linn Grove, they found the craft on the ground, came within 700 m of it but it *"spread its four giant wings and rose towards the North."* Two strange figures aboard the craft made efforts to conceal themselves. Witnesses were surprised at the length of their hair. Most residents of Linn Grove saw the craft in flight.[79]

15th April 1897 Howard-Artesian, South Dakota. A flying object at nightfall coming closer and closer to the ground followed a train, as reported by the engineer, Joe Wright.[80]

15th April 1897 Perry Springs, Missouri. A passenger train on the Wabash line, going towards Quincy, was followed by a low-flying object for 15 minutes between Perry Springs and Hersman. All the passengers saw the craft, which had a red and white light. After Hersman, it flew ahead of the train and disappeared rapidly, although the train was then running at 65 km/h.[81]

15th April 1897 Springfield, Illinois. Two farm workers, Adolph Winkle and John Hulle, saw a strange craft in a field. They had a discussion with its occupants, a woman and two men, and were told the ship had flown from Quincy to Springfield in 30 minutes and that the crew was making electrical repairs.[82]

16th April 1897 Downs Township, Illinois. Approximate date. While working in his field, Haney Savidge saw an aerial craft land near him. Six people emerged from it and spoke to him for a few minutes, before leaving again.[83]

17th April 1897 Williamston, Michigan. At least a dozen farmers in the morning saw an object manoevre in the sky for an hour before it landed. A strange man near 3 metres tall, almost naked and suffering from the heat, was the pilot of the craft. *"His talk, while musical, seemed to be a repetition of bellowings."* One farmer went near him and received a blow that broke his hip.[84]

20th April 1897 Homan, Arkansas. Capt. James Hooton was hunting in the vicinity of Homan, when he heard the noise of a steam engine and found an object in a clearing. It looked like a cylinder with pointed ends, lateral wheels and a horizontal blade over it. Hooton spoke with a man who wore dark glasses and walked behind the craft. There were three or four occupants. The witness was told this was indeed 'The Airship' and that it used compressed air for propulsion. Hooton saw the wheels spin as the craft rose and flew away. Depicted below, is a sketch of the 'airship' seen by Captain James Hooton at Homan, Arkansas.[85]

22nd April 1897 Rockland, Texas. John M. Barclay was intrigued when his dog barked furiously and a high-pitched noise was heard. He went out and saw a flying object circling 5 m above ground. Elongated, with protrusions and blinding lights, it went dark when it landed. Barclay was met by a man who told him his purpose was peaceful and requested some common hardware items to repair the craft. He paid with a ten-dollar bill and took off *"like a bullet out of a gun."*[86]

22nd April 1897 Josserand, Texas. Frank Nichols, who lived 3 km east of Josserand and was one of its most respected citizens, was awakened by a machine noise. Looking outside, he saw a heavy, lighted object land in his wheat field. He walked towards it and was stopped by two men who asked permission to draw water from his well. He then had a discussion with a half-dozen men, the crew of the strange machine. He was told how it worked but could not follow the explanation.[87]

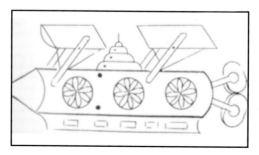

23rd April 1897 McKinney Bayou, Arkansas. Judge Lawrence of Texarkana, Arkansas, was surveying a tract of land when he saw a peculiar object anchored on the ground. *"It was manned by three men who spoke a foreign language, but judging from their looks one would take them to be Japs."* [88]

25th April 1897 Merkel, Texas. People returning from church in the evening surveyed a heavy object being dragged along the ground by a rope attached to a flying craft. The rope got caught in a railroad track. The craft was too high for its structure to be visible but protrusions and a light could be distinguished. After about 10 minutes a man came down along the rope cut the end free and went back aboard the craft, which flew away toward the northeast. The man was small and dressed in a light blue uniform.[89]

26th April 1897 Aquila-Hillsboro, Texas. Approximate date. A lawyer was surprised to see a lighted object fly over. His horse was scared and nearly toppled the carriage. When the main light was turned off, a number of smaller lights became visible on the underside of the dark object, which supported an elongated canopy. It went down towards a hill to the south, 5 km from Aquila. When the witness was on his way back one hour later, he saw the object rising. It reached the altitude of the cloud ceiling and flew to the northeast at a fantastic speed, with periodic flashes of light.[90]

6th May 1897 Hot Springs, Arkansas. Two policemen, Sumpter and McLenore, were riding northwest of Hot Springs when they saw a bright light in the sky. About 7 km further they saw the light again coming down to the ground. One km further the horses refused to walk. Two men were seen carrying lights. The lawmen took their rifles, called the strangers and were told that they crossed the country with a flying craft. The silhouette of the machine, about 20 m long, could be seen in the clearing. There was a woman with an umbrella nearby. It was raining, and the younger of the men was filling a large container with water. The elder man had a beard and suggested that the policemen fly with them *"to a place where it does not rain."* The same witness went back through the same spot 40 minutes later and found nothing.[91]

1898 A professor Michailovitch, of the Belgrade Observatory followed a 'comet', which stayed motionless in the sky for six minutes.[92]

CHAPTER CONCLUSION

These one hundred plus accounts form only a small fraction of historical UFO sightings from around the world. What are we to make of these accounts? Do they all have a natural explanation? We should bear in mind that they were written before the development of aircraft, the cultural contamination of television and the media, and the majority before the invention of hot air balloons. Could they be clever works of fiction? Like many sightings today, a number of these accounts had multiple witnesses or were recorded by articulate individuals. Maybe we should keep an open mind?

SOURCES

1) Cicero, *Of the Nature of the Gods*, Book I, Ch. 2
2) Livy, *History*, Book VIII, Ch. 11
3) Dio Cassius, *Roman History*, Book 1
4) Pliny, *Natural History*, Book II, Ch. 32
5) Livy, *History*, Books XXI-XXII
6) Livy, *History*, Book XXII, Ch. 1
7) J Obsequens, *Liber Prodigiorum, Chapter 31*, note n. 81
8) Ibid, Ch. 66
9) Ibid, Ch 114
10) Ibid. Ch.114
11) Ibid, *Chapter 105*, note 486, 488, 490
12) Ibid, *Chapter 105*, note 486, 488, 490
13) From Pliny, *Natural History Book II*, Ch 34
14) Obsequens, *Prodigiorum*, Ch. 114
15) Extract from the *Military Records of General Luculus* written by Plutarchus.
16) Pliny, *Natural History, Book II*, Ch. 35
17) Dio Cassius, *Roman History, Book IV*
18) Obsequens, *Prodigiorum*, Ch. 130
19) Josephus, *Jewish War*, box CXI
20) Conrad Wolfhart, Lycothenes. Prodigiorum Ac Ostentorum
21) Ibid
22) *Acta Sanctorum*, Volume 2.
23) *Historia ecclesiastica gentis Anglorum*, Bede
24) Drake, W. R. *Did UFOs Stop A War?* p13 FSR, IX, No 2 March-April 1963.
25) Vallee, Jacques; *Passport to Magonia* .
26) *Ribera El gran enigma*, p356
27) Vallee, Jacques; *Passport to Magonia* p.6
28) Vallee, Jacques; *UFO's in Space: Anatomy of a Phenomenon*, p.9
29) *The Journal* (newspaper), 23 August, 1985, page 4
30) Vallee, Jacques; *Passport to Magonia*, pp.4-5
31) Ibid, p.5
32) Bulletin of the CBA Association (Yokohoma) III,1(1964)
33) Vallee, Jacques; *Passport to Magonia*, p.6
34) Raphael Holinshed, Holinshed's *Chronicles of England, Scotland and Ireland*. Six volumes. London: Printed for J. Johnson, 1808. The account appears in the second volume, page 829.
35) Jacques Vallee, *Passport to Magonia*, p 6
36) Jacques Vallee, *UFO's in Space: Anatomy of a Phenomenon*, p.9; Harold T. Wilkins, *Flying Saucers on the Attack*, pp.187-88
37) Vallee, Jacques; *Passport to Magonia*, pp.5-6
38) cf. Letopisetul Moldovcenesc
39) Armand/Holm-Hansen: *UFOER OVER NORGE*, 1971, 73.
40) Viage al estrecho de Magallanes por el Capitán Pedro Sarmiento..." 1768
41) Jacques Vallee, *Passport to Magonia* p6
42) *Discours Espouventable. Des Signes Qui Sont Apparus sur la mer de Gennes* - Pierre Menier 1608
43) *Histoires de la Fin du Monde*. By Marc Deceneux P111
44) *Biblioteca Academiei*, "manuscris slavon" 706.
45) The first image is from *Lettres edifantes et curieuses Tolosa 1811*, tomo XIV page 197; the second is from *Der Neue Welt Bolt* (n.226).
46) *Mysteries of the Unexplianed*, Reader's Digest Association, February 1985, p 210
47) *Biblioteca Academiei*, "manuscris românesc" 2342, f. 3-4
48) Vallee, Jacques; *Passport to Magonia* p 6
49) Ibid, p7
50) *Biblioteca Romänesc* 2150, f. 111v.
51) *Biblioteca Academiei, manuscris românesc* 1346 f:2V.
52) Ion Hobana & Julien Weverbergh, *UFOs Behind The Iron Curtain* 1972
53) Ibid

54) *Biblioteca Academiei, Manuscris românesc* 4043, f.1 and *Albina românescâ*, pp. 81-82

55) Original newspaper article in the National Library of Madrid. Friday August 14th 1863 edition, issue number 226, in a section headed *INTERIOR*

56) Chalker, W 1982, *A UFO Vision: The Mystery of a Machine to Go through the Air,* in UFORAN 3(1):14-26).

57) Vallee, Jacques;, *Anatomy of a Phenomenon*

58) The Books of Charles Fort 189

59) Source Robin Northover, Post

60) Vallee, Jacques; *Anatomy of a Phenomenon*

61) *Roundup 17; Anatomy 12*

62) Vallee, Jacques; *Passport to Magonia*

63) *Lorenzen III 2O6*

64) *Flying Saucer Review* 65, 3

65) *Le Livre des damnés*, p. 234

66) The Books of Charles Fort 637

67) *Lumières dans la Nuit* 48

68) Ibid, 48

69) *The Australian*, 14-16 May 1969

70) Crowley, A; *Magic Without Tears.*

71) From the *San Francisco Call*, Nov 26, 1896

72) *Flying Saucer Review* 66, 4

73) *Chicago Times-Herald*, Mar. 30, 1897

74) *Flying Saucer Review* 66, 4

75) *Chicago Times-Herald*, Apr. 14, 1897

76) *Chicago Times-Herald*, April 14, 1897, *Chicago Record*, April 14, 1897

77) *Chicago Chronicle*, Apr. 15, 1897

78) *Chicago Tribune*, Apr. 16, 1897

79) *Chicago Times-Herald*, Apr. 16, 1897

80) *Flying Saucer Review* 66,4

81) *Chicago Times-Herald*, Apr. 16, 1897

82) *Flying Saucer Review* 65,1

83) *Chicago Times-Herald*, Apr. 16, 1897

84) *Lansing State Republican*, Apr. 1897

85) *Flying Saucer Review* 66, 4

86) Vallee, Jacques; *Passport to Magonia*

87) Ibid p89

88) Farish, in Allende Letters (Award Special, 1968)

89) Vallee, Jacques; *Passport to Magonia*

90) *Dallas Morning News*, Apr. 28, 1897

91) *Flying Saucer Review* 66, 4

92) Vallee, Jacques; *Anatomy of a Phenomenon* p. 35

OUT OF PLACE ARTIFACTS *Chapter Seven*

OUT OF PLACE ARTIFACTS
OUT OF PLACE ARTIFACTS

Around the world a number of objects or artifacts have been discovered, which possess a high degree of technology outside the time frame of their creation. The implication is that ancient man possessed advanced knowledge, far more than the orthodoxy today would give them credit for. This leads to the question, from where did they obtain this ancient wisdom?

THE NAZCA LINES

Located in an area of 200 miles south of Lima, Peru is a plain 37 miles long and a mile wide. But this is no ordinary plain. It became the canvas for some form of intelligence to create a series of lines, geometric forms and animals, some of which are only visible from the air at a height of 1100 ft. They were discovered in 1926 by archaeologists Alfred Kroeber and Toribio Mejia Xesspe. Consequently, as air routes opened up, more and more pilots reported strange markings on the ground. The designs come in two forms: biomorphs - which consist of some 70 animal and plant figures estimated to have been created around 200 BC. Secondly, geoglyphs,

Figure 1) The Nazca Lines (below and left): Two photographs of the many lines found at Nazca. The one below stretches for over five miles.

© Erich Von Däniken

The photograph on the opposite page is of a strange suited-six-fingered entity found in Kiev dated to 4000 BC.

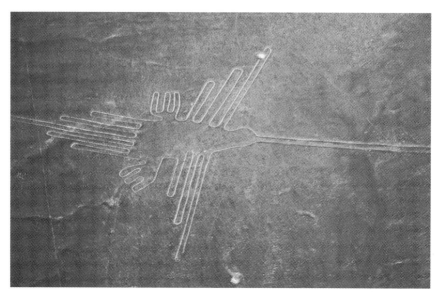

which are geometric forms that include straight lines, triangles, spirals and circles totalling some 900, thought to be constructed around 300 AD. They were created by clearing the surface stones to form lines, thus exposing the lighter (sub-surface) sand underneath. Due to the fact the location is one of the driest on the Earth, there has been little erosion over time.

Since those initial discoveries in 1929, they've become a 'Mecca' for tourists and theorists alike. Arguably the best-known researcher of the lines was German mathematician Maria Reiche. She spent half a Century researching the glyphs and came to the conclusion the lines were based on astronomical alignments. This was, however, disproved in the 1960s by an American astronomer, who concluded that the number of lines that were astronomically significant was no more than pure chance.[1]
Probably the most famous and well known theory is Erich Von Däniken's idea that the lines served as landing strips for ancient astronauts. Von Däniken consequently withdrew this theory, exclaiming it was an editorial error and said they were instead a 'signal' to the Gods.

Another theory is that the lines and symbols served as religious centres. Some lines pointed to mountains, where according to Native American tradition, water or rain Gods lived. Broken pottery and stone piles have been found in some of these areas.
A more recent idea put forward is that the markings are related to shamanism, whereby the shamans mapped out a kind of spirit landscape in an altered state of consciousness. One thing is for sure, due to their size they were designed to be noticed from the air and the artists either used scale drawings, or were directed by intelligences from above!
Ultimately no one really knows why they were made but one can still marvel at the sheer size and beauty of these glyphs in Peru.[2]

THE MITCHELL HEDGES CRYSTAL SKULL

The author first came across this artifact when he saw an episode of Arthur C Clarke's series back in 1981. I was amazed at the anatomical precision of the skull shown. Due to its undoubted accuracy and perfection, I have decided to include it in this chapter. There are in actual fact a number of crystal skulls around the world.

The Mitchell Hedges is the most famous and impressive. It is named after its finder, an Englishman Frederick A Mitchell Hedges. The story goes that he led an expedition in 1924 to find evidence for the civilisation of Atlantis. What he did find was this crystal skull buried beneath an altar in a ruined Mayan temple in Lubaantun. The jaw was allegedly found 3 months later 25ft away. It weighs 11.7 pounds, is 5 inches high and 5 inches wide. Because of its small size, it is thought to resemble a female skull. There are around twelve other crystal skulls around the world in museums and private collections. One is housed in the Museum of Mankind in London and a smaller one in the Musee de l'Homme in Paris.

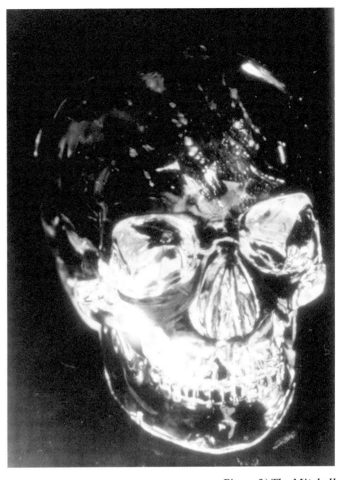

Figure 3) The Mitchell Hedges Crystal Skull (above):

© *The Fortean Picture Library*

Whatever the truth behind the discovery of the object, what is for certain is that it is an anatomically perfect replica of a human skull, complete with detachable jawbone and 32 teeth. What is really amazing about the skull is that it is carved from a single piece of quartz with no tooling marks! Hewlett-Packard carried out tests in 1970 and their conclusion was: *"if it's phony, it's a very artistic one, the workmanship is exquisite."* [3] They were perplexed at how a primitive culture could have carved crystal into such precise shapes, especially against the natural axis of the crystal. Crystal is a substance that has a perfect symmetry of how its molecules align. When a carver cuts crystal, the crystal will shatter if carved against the axis. Hewlett-Packard were able to establish that the crystal skull had been made from a particular type of quartz, known as 'piezo electric silicon dioxide' - precisely the type of quartz that is now used throughout the modern electronics industry. Unlike other materials, the quartz used to make the skull has the ability to hold under control electrical energy. It is able to hold electrical energy, potentially a form of information, and send out impulses, or vibrating waves of information.

What was the skull used for? According to legends of the American natives, crystal skulls were used to get into telepathic contact with their 'Gods' in order to receive knowledge and wisdom. Here we have another relic from the past proving that mankind was once in possession of objects we would have trouble replicating with today's technology.

MYSTERIOUS MAPS

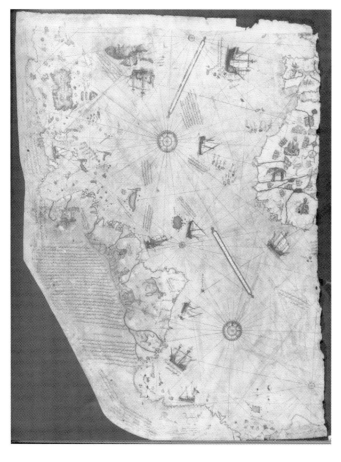

Our next exhibit is a map from 1513, known as the Piri Reis Map. It was discovered in 1929, wrapped up on a shelf at the Old Imperial Palace, Turkey. It is named after the Turkish Cartographer, Admiral Piri Reis. What is unusual about this map is that it depicts the landmass of Antarctica, not officially discovered until 1818. More bizarrely, it depicts Antarctica free of ice!

Where did Piri Reis obtain his information? He claims to have met a sailor who obtained maps from Columbus. Columbus in turn made them from an old book dating back to Alexander the Great, probably from the Imperial Library in Constantinople, and they were probably transferred from even more ancient documents.

Also depicted is the correct position of the Falkland Islands, not discovered until 1592, and also the rivers of South America, Orinoco, Amazon and Panama.

The late Professor Hapgood, after studying the map determined that: *"...the evidence presented by the*

Figure 4)
The Piri Reis Map
(above):
© *The Turkish National Museum*

ancient maps appears to suggest the existence in remote times, before the rise of any of the known cultures, of a true civilisation, of a comparatively advanced sort, which either was localised in one area but had worldwide commerce, or was, in a real sense, a worldwide culture."[4]

Hapgood showed the map to the US reconnaissance technical squadron, their reply stated: *"...the geographical detail shown in the lower part of the map agrees very remarkably with the results of the seismic profile made across the top of the ice cap by the Swedish- British Antarctic Expedition of 1949."*

"We have no idea how the data on this map can be reconciled with the supposed state of geographical knowledge in 1513."

Hapgood also put forward a theory that Antarctica remained free of ice as late as 4000 BC. He called this theory Earth Crust Displacement, the idea being that the Earth's crust shifted, causing Antarctica to move south from an ice-free position to its current position and become glaciated.

Prior to investigating the map Hapgood presented his idea of a global geological theory to Einstein. His abridged reply was:

"His idea is original, of great simplicity, and if it continues to prove itself - of great importance to everything that is related to the history of the Earth's surface."

Researcher, Charles Hapgood, made the following comments about the Oronteus Finaeus map after spending many hours looking for an ancient map of Antarctica in the Reference Room of the Library of Congress, Washington DC. His comments sum up the map pretty well.

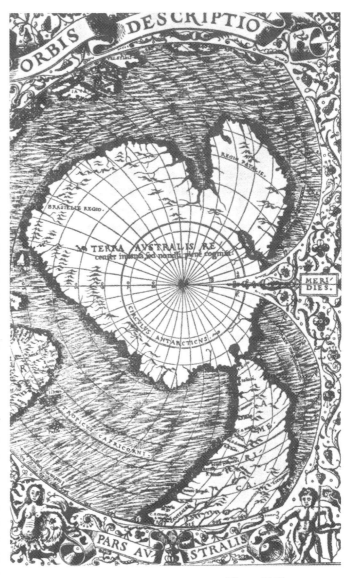

Figure 5) The Oronteus Finaeus:
Another map of interest is the Oronteus Finaeus, showing Antarctica with ice-free coasts, mountains and rivers. The Antarctica part is shown above.

" I found many fascinating things I had not expected to find, and a number of charts showing the southern continent. Then, one day, I turned a page and sat transfixed. As my eyes fell upon the southern hemisphere of a world map drawn by Oronteus Finaeus in 1531, I had the instant conviction that I had found here a truly authentic map of the real Antarctica.
"The general shape of the continent was startlingly like the outline of the continent on our modern maps. The position of the South Pole, nearly in the centre of the continent, seemed about right. The mountain ranges that skirted the coasts suggested the numerous ranges that have been discovered in Antarctica in recent

years. It was obvious too, that this was no slapdash creation of somebody's imag-ination. The mountain ranges were individualised, some definitely coastal and some not. From most of them, rivers were shown flowing into the sea, following in every case what looked like very natural and very convincing drainage pat-terns. This suggested, of course, that the coasts might have been ice-free when the original was drawn. The deep interior, however, was free entirely of rivers and mountains, suggesting that the ice might have been present there."[5]

Dr Richard Strachan of the Massachusetts Institute of Technology, confirmed that the map had been copied and compiled from a number of

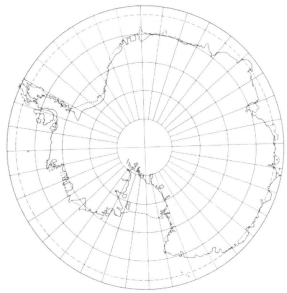

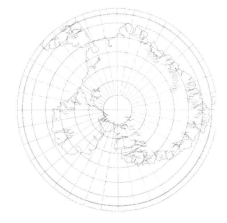

earlier source maps, it did indeed show non-glacial areas of Antarctica, including Queen Maud Land, Enderby Land, Wilkes Land and Victoria Land and finally, as with the Piri Reis Map, the general profile matched closely seismic survey maps of the sub glacial-surfaces of Antarctica.

To conclude, we have two astonishing maps that not only show Antarctica several hundred years before its official discovery, but also free of ice. What is the implication of this? First of all it demonstrates that sometime in the history of the Earth, before at least the 1500's, a seafaring people existed that could circumnavigate the globe and accurately survey its features. Secondly, it raises the question, if the ice cap has been in place for millions years how was this accomplished?

Did the maps originate prior to this time? Was it mapped while the ice caps were in place? Is the ice cap development actually a much more recent event than we think?

THE GREAT PYRAMID

The Great Pyramid, according to orthodoxy, was built as a tomb for the Pharaoh Khufu in c.2500 BC. The mathematical precision in this monu-ment is astounding, I felt the best way to illustrate this is in a series of bul-let points:

* It's 500 ft high and the base covers 13 acres.
* Each side precisely faces the four points of the compass, with only 1/12th of a degree variation.
* If the height is divided into the radius of the Earth and the perimeter into the circumference: 365.256 and 365.259 are arrived at respectively. 365 days is the number of days for the Earth to revolve around the Sun.
* The sides rise at 52 degrees. The significance of this is that only at this angle is the ratio of the height to the base equal to PI.
* The descending passage is 150 ft and there is only a deviation of 1/50th of an inch.
* 2.3 million blocks of yellow limestone compose the majority of the pyramid, mostly weighing 2.5 tons each.
* They fit together so well that no mortar was used.
* Some of the interior blocks are made of granite and weigh 60-70 tons.
* The granite blocks originally came from a quarry in Aswan some 600 miles away!
* The pyramid was originally cased in white limestone up to untill 500 BC, after which it was stripped off and used in the construction of mosques.
* 115,000 of these six sided stones were used weighing 10 tons, polished and precision carved to fit perfectly with each other, with joints measuring less than 1/50th of an inch.
* They would have powerfully reflected sunlight and made the pyramid visible for hundreds of miles.
* The weight of the pyramid is 6-7 million tons and its mass 90 million cubic feet.
* The pyramid's base is less than 22 inches thick yet almost perfectly level, with a deviation of 1 inch across the entire area.
* The Pyramid is located at the exact centre of the Earth's landmass. That is, its East-West axis corresponds to the longest land parallel across the Earth, passing through Africa, Asia and America. Similarly, the longest land meridian on Earth, through Asia, Africa, Europe and Antarctica, also passes right

through the pyramid. Since the Earth has enough land area to provide three billion possible building sites for the Pyramid, the odds of it having been built where it is are 1 in 3 billion.

So there we have a number of thought provoking facts and figures about the Great Pyramid. A number of experts have examined the Great Pyramid; Sir WF Petrie, an eminent archeologist commented:

"merely to place such stones in exact contact would be careful work, but to do so with cement in the joints seems almost impossible, it is to be compared with the finest opticians work on a scale of acres."[6]

The Kings chamber contains a granite coffer hewn out of a single piece of solid granite. Petrie stated that diamond tipped drills with a pressure of two tons would be required. Chris Dunn, an English engineer examined the pyramid and concluded that the only possible method of machining the granite would have been ultrasonic machinery.

Having digested all of the above, we are faced with the question, just how was it built? The orthodox idea is that ramps were used, built of brick and earth. It has been calculated that a ramp constructed so as to reach the top of the pyramid with a 1: 10 gradient would have to be 4,800 ft long! Many engineers feel the ramp would have caved in under the weight. Also, how do you house, feed and water the many slaves that would have been required? Greek historian, Herodotus, reckoned it would take 100,000 slaves 30 years to complete and that is forgetting the almost supernatural engineering precision.

Another conundrum is that according to the official line, it was constructed within a very early part of the Egyptian civilisation. From humble beginnings, the Egyptians must have amassed knowledge of surveying, geometry, construction techniques and large-scale project management to enable them to go from no building to the Khufu pyramid in less than 600 years. Either they were far more intelligent than we are today, or they had existing knowledge that came from somewhere. Many feel it is impossible to develop the knowledge needed, in that time frame, to build pyramids of that size and precision. Interestingly, later Egyptian pyramids fail to match the quality of construction and precision of the Great Pyramid; how was this knowledge suddenly lost?

Why was it built? The official explanation, as a tomb, has a number of holes in it. This idea has its origins in Herodotus who visited the Giza plateau in 500 BC and wrote that he was informed by tour guides that it was built as a tomb. Since that day Egyptologists have accepted this statement as fact![7]

When the Kings chamber (which contains the granite coffer) was opened in 1818, no body was found and no mention of Khufu is recorded anywhere in or on the pyramid except for some graffiti discovered in 1837. An inscription at Giza, the Inventory Stele mentions Isis as the *"Mistress of the Pyramid."* No mention of Khufu! Isis, a 'star goddess' goes back to the beginning of Egyptian legend and history and she can be found in various ancient civilisations under other names. Ashtarte (Phoenician) and Ishtar (Sumerian) are just two examples.

Many other theories as to its purpose have been put forward including a water pump, a stellar observatory, a beacon for visiting spaceships and a temple. Here we have another relic from the past, awesome engineering precision, mysterious origins and function.

ANCIENT ASTRONAUTS ?

Below is a collection of artifacts from around the world that seem to depict men in helmets and protective suits. In fact, they look remarkably like space suits! Critics point out they are simply examples of native rit-

8

ual costumes. This figure (top right) was discovered on the Ecuador/Bolivia border. It is 30 cm in height and estimated to be 3000 years old. *See figure 8 (top right).*

Figure 9) far left:
http://www.geocities.com/t
asosmit2001/Ancientmyste
ries/Astronaut1.jpg

Figure 10) left:
©http://marcogee.free.fr/ov
ni/ancosmo.html

Figure 11) centre left:
These ancient South American figures appear to be wearing protective helmets.
http://www.geocities.com/t
asosmit2001/Ancientmyste
ries/helmet.jpg

Figure 12) left:
More examples of suited figures from South America.

11)http://marcogee.free.fr/o
vni/ancosmo.html
12)http://marcogee.free.fr/o
vni/ancosmo.html
Courtesy of
www.daniken.com
© Erich Von Däniken

Figures 13* and *14 (above):
The two photos above depict artifacts found in South America, estimated to be 1000 years old.

Figure 15 *(left): A comparison of one artifact found in Peru with an Apollo Astronaut.*

Figure 16 (opposite page):
On the top far right is a head from Periodica, Kosovo, Serbia, Federal Republic of Yugoslavia, c. 4500-4000 BC. Clay, seven inches (17.8 cm) high.

All photographs Courtesy of Erich Von Däniken
© www.daniken.com

Figure 16 (below):
This artifact looks similar to what many people today would call a Grey alien

©http://www.sarajevo.net/ alienmuseum/

Figure 17 (left):
The cover art for Whitley Strieber's best-seller
Communion.

© Whitely Strieber
© Cover art courtesy of Ted Seth Jacobs

Figure 18 (below):
This photograph is of a strange suited-six-fingered entity and was found in Kiev dated to 4000 BC.

Figures 19 & 20 (left): These ceramic figures (known as Dogu statues) were made by a Neolithic people from Japan called the Jomon. They apparently were the first people on Earth to make clay pottery. Their figures according to R-14 dating, go back as far as 12,000 years. Orthodox scientists regard them as fertility objects or funeral depictions. To researcher, Vaughn Green, they represent an ancient artifact depicting men in space suits. He claims to have found 30 points of similarity with a space suit including rivets, rubber cuffs, chest controls, safety straps etc. One can clearly see there is a commonality with the South American figures - that of space suited beings. Could the Jomons have been replicating the 'sky Gods' they may have witnessed? Or where they themselves connected to these strange alien-like creatures?[8]

Figure 21 (below):
This 3,000-year-old
object was found in
Toprakkale, Turkey.
It looks remarkably
like a space module
with a pilot sitting
(whose head is miss-
ing) at controls.
© Istanbul
Archaeology Museum
in Turkey.

ANCIENT AIRCRAFT

For several decades, aeroplane-like objects have been on display at the Gold Museum, Bogotá. These artifacts (below) were excavated 30 years ago and are believed to have come from the Sinu culture, a pre-Incan civilisation dating between the Sixth and Ninth Centuries AD. They are 5 cms long and made of gold, have tail fins, broad triangular wings and an open area where a cockpit would be. Critics say they are just stylised depictions of insects but as Von Däniken points out, there are no insect cults in South America. Algund Eenboom concluded the 'wings' of all insects are attached at the top of the corpus, not at the bot-

Figure 22 & 23 (below)
Artifacts from the
Gold Museum,
Bogotá

tom. Friends of Von Däniken, Eeenboom and Belting decided to build a scale model based on one of these objects to determine if it could fly.

The team and one of the scale models. Belting made a model plane, first with a propeller, afterwards with a jet engine. Whereas the first had to be launched by hand, the jet engine one was also equipped with landing gear. The results were a great success, both flew without a hitch!

As well as in South America, another ancient aircraft like object was found in a tomb in Saqqara, Egypt in 1898. Dated to 200 BC, it has the inscription 'gift of Amon', the God of the wind. It is seven inches long and made of light sycamore wood and weighs only 1.11 ounces. [9]

It seems both the South Americans and the Egyptians predated knowledge of aerodynamics by many centuries!

All photographs courtesy of:
www.daniken.com
www.-user.rhrk.uni-kl.de/~aws/seta/Triebwerke

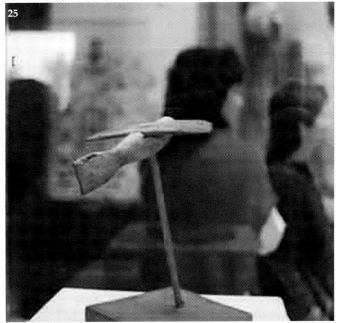

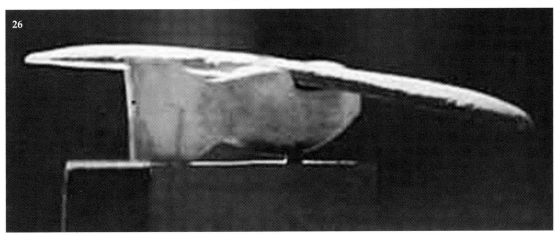

THE BAGHDAD BATTERY

Another curious artifact from the past is an object which has become known as 'The Baghdad Battery'. The object first came to prominence in 1938, when German archeologist Wilhelm Konig first wrote about it. No one is sure if Konig unearthed the object or whether he discovered it in the vaults of the National Museum of Iraq. What is known is that the object was originally discovered in Khujut Rabu, near Baghdad.

On first inspection it resembles an earthenware jar, about the size of a man's fist. At the top of the jar is an asphalt stopper, protruding from this is an iron rod. The iron rod runs through the jar and is surrounded by a copper shield. Konig was convinced it was a primitive form of battery. American Willard FM Gray, followed up on Konig's findings and built some replicas. When filled with an electrolyte like grape juice, the objects produced two volts.

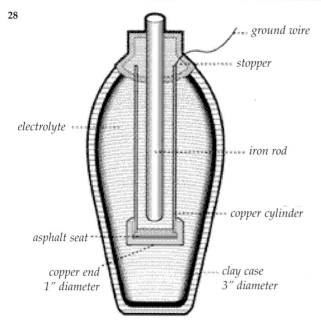

ground wire
stopper
electrolyte
iron rod
copper cylinder
asphalt seat
copper end
1" diameter
clay case
3" diameter

Figures 27 and 28 (Above):
© The Baghdad Museum

Traditionally, Count Alessandro Volta invented the battery in 1800. The term Volt stems from his surname after his discovery. We have an object, however, that is 2,000 years old producing volts! It appears Volta was beaten to it! A number of questions now arise: Who built it? Why was it built?

To answer the first question, we have to travel to where the object was originally found - Khujut Rabu. This area was inhabited by a group of people known as the Porthians. They had not been noted for their technological prowess and it is considered unlikely that they invented it. We are then left with the idea that it was introduced by an outside source, but whom? Could it have been developed by accident? German researcher, Dr Arne Eggebrecht, has come up with the idea that it was used to electroplate items. Eggebrecht used copies of the battery to test this idea. She suggests that many ancient items in museums that are thought to be gold, may actually be gold-plated silver! [10]

THE GREEK COMPUTER

Amongst the treasures of the Greek National Archeological Museum in Athens, is a device which has become known as the Antikythera Device or the Greek Computer.

In 1900, a sponge diver located a wreck off the Island of Antikythera, midway between Crete and Kythera. When the contents of this wreck were brought to the surface, amongst the finds was a corroded bronze instrument, caked in calcareous deposits. After cleaning and closer exam-

ination, experts determined the object was an ancient navigational tool - an Astrolabe.

The object received intensive examination in 1951 by Professor Derek de Solla Price, of Yale University. He and his team subjected the object to a series of X-rays and gamma rays to examine its internal structure. His conclusion was astonishing, the device was a 2000-year-old analogue computer designed to mimic past, present and future movements of the sun, moon and planets.

How was the object dated? An epigrapher, Benjamin Dean Meritt dated the characters from the inscriptions found on the object to c. 100 BC. Price determined the original mechanism consisted of a rectangular box about twelve inches by six by three inches, with the bronze machinery contained by wooden sides. Bronze doors on which the inventor had inscribed detailed instructions covered the front and back. Three dials displayed the device's readout. The first dial contained two concentric

Figure 29 (above):
The corroded remains of the Antikythera mechanism.
© The Greek Archeolgical Museum
See also:
http://www.culture.gr/2/21/214/21405m/00/lm05m04c.jpg

bands, one showed the signs of the zodiac, a sixteen-degree-wide belt straddling the apparent path of the sun, and the other the names of the Greek months. A pointer showed the position of the sun in the zodiac for every day of the year. A second dial displayed an eighteen-year cycle of solar eclipses, while a third showed the phases of the moon. Inside, thirty-nine bronze gears were set in motion by a handle that needed to be turned once a day. A differential gear was used in the mechanism, which had been thought to be a Seventeenth Century development.

The identity of the machine's inventor is unknown. Some scholars believe it has its origins on the island of Rhodes. It seems the Antikythera mechanism is representative of a large body of knowledge from the Hellenistic era. What other knowledge and devices did the ancient Greeks possess? Are there any more wondrous artifacts lying on the bottom of the Aegean Sea that may revise our knowledge of history? [11]

SOURCES

1) In 1973, Dr Gerald Hawkins studied 186 lines with a computer programme and found that only 20 per cent had any astronomical orientation - again no more than by pure chance.

2) *X-Factor Magazine* volume 4, issue 40 pp1107-1111. *X Factor Magazine.* An eight-volume magazine on the unexplained published between 1995-1999 by Marshall Cavendish Ltd. 119 Wardour Street, London W1V 3TD.

http://www.unmuseum.org/nazca.htm
http://www.crystalinks.com/nasca.html
http://www.eridu.co.uk/eridu/Author/Mysteries_of_the_World/Nazca/nazca.html

3) *X Factor volume 4,* issue 48, pp1336-1340
"In 1964, Anna Mitchell-Hedges lent the skull to Frank Dorland, an art conservator. He ran a series of tests on it over a period of six years and concluded that the skull is "the grand daddy of all crystal balls". He told Richard Garvin, author of The Crystal Skull, that he had seen a glowing aura around the skull and that while it was in his house, he often heard "human voices singing some strange chants in a very soft voice." Dorland and Garvin allowed the electronics company Hewlett-Packard to conduct laser tests on the skull in 1970. Their conclusion, was "if its phony, it's a very artistic one... the workmanship is exquisite, a compound of patient hand crafting and technical precision requiring an estimated 300 man years of effort."

4) Hapgood, Dr. Charles; *Maps of the Ancient Sea Kings; Evidence of Advanced Civilization in the Ice Age.* Chilton Books. Philadelphia and New York 1966.

5) Ibid

6) Hancock, Graham; *Fingerprints of the Gods.* William Heinmann. Chapter 6.

7) *Gods of the New Millennium.* Alan Alford Eridu Books 1996 Chapter 9

8) For further information on the Dogu read *The Six-Thousand-Year-Old Spacesuit* by Vaughn M Green. Merlin Engine Works 1982.

9) For further reading consult *Arrival of the Gods*. Erich Von Däniken. Element Books 1998.

10) *http://www.unmuseum.org/bbattery.htm*. The unmuseum.org - a well designed and informative website by Lee Krystek covering a multitude of mysteries.

11) *http://www.world-mysteries.com/sar_4.htm*. *World-Mysteries.com* is a non profit web site. Covering subjects such as lost civilisations, ancient ruins, sacred writings, unexplained artifacts and science mysteries. Introduced are 'alternative theories', subject experts, books and resources on the Internet.

UFOs DEPICTED IN EARLY PHOTOGRAPHY
Chapter Eight

With the advent of photography in the first half of the Nineteenth Century, it was only a matter of time before photographs of UFOs started to appear. Photographs of UFOs prior to 1950, however, are exceedingly rare; therefore the compilation in this chapter represents a summation of the author's research into known images.
1947 was considered to be an apt cut-off point as this pre-dates Kenneth Arnold's sighting and the Roswell incident; both famous cases that have given Ufology a starting point. Some of the photos documented here involved multiple witnesses.

Figure 1) **1870-1871 (left):**
This photograph depicts a cloud formation over the summit of Mt. Washington in the winter of 1870 - 1871 - along with an added surprise! One can see a cigar-shaped object. This could possibly be the earliest photograph of a UFO. The image is part of an antique stereo view. The description on the stereo view read: *"SUMMIT Mt. Washington WINTER 1870-1871. Entered according to Act of Congress in the year 1871, by CLOGH & KIMBALL, in the Office of the Librarian of Congress, at Washington."*

Figure 2) **1883 (** *on the next page***):**
This early UFO photograph was taken on the 12th August 1883. Astronomer Jose Bonilla, at Zacatecas Observatory, Mexico whilst observing the Sun, photographed formations of 'elongated objects moving in pairs over the Sun's disc.' He estimated the objects to be no higher than 300,000 kilometres. Bonilla sent his photographic plates to *L'Astronomie*, a French publication, where they were accepted and eventually included on page 347 of the 1885 volume. This is what Bonilla himself wrote in this

*The negative on the opposite page shows a UFO that was featured in the **Los Angeles Times** on the 25th February 1942.*

journal, specialising in popular astronomy, meteorology and Globe physics and published by Camille Flammarion:

"At 8.00 am on 12th August, 1883 I had begun to single out some solar points when, suddenly, I noticed a small bright object entering the telescope field and showing on the paper I was using to mark the points. It then crossed the Sun's disc, casting an almost circular shadow. I was stunned with surprise. I was only beginning to get over it when the same phenomenon repeated itself so very frequently that, in the next two hours, I was able to count as many as 283 objects crossing the Sun's face."

Bonilla and his helper managed to sight a total of 331 objects on August 12th (divided into two different periods of 283 and 48 objects respectively) and then 116 objects on the following day. That is, 447 UFOs altogether. The trajectory described by the objects was west-east, somehow moving towards the north or the south of the Sun's disc.

"...I had been observing them for a few minutes, says the head of the Zacatecas Observatory, when I noticed those bodies -some of which were perfectly round, whereas others had an elongated shape- looked black and somber while projecting themselves through the Sun's disc, but then looked luminous when they moved away from the Sun across the telescope field. As I used to take frequent photographs of the Sun when its disc was showing spots and 'faculae', that is, luminous areas in the Sun's photosphere, easily perceived near the Sun's edge, I consequently decided to take some pictures of this odd, interesting phenomenon showing a number of bodies flying across the Sun. In order to do so, I removed the 16-cm lens from the equatorial and put in another lens of exactly the same intensity, fitted with a chemical focus (suitable for photographic work), as well as a photo camera in the eyepiece. After several attempts to adjust the equipment I managed to take some photographs, eventually sending the most interesting-looking one to L'Astronomie. While I was taking these photographs, a helper was using the equatorial discoverer of the telescope to count the bodies. The picture was taken by using a wet plate with 1/100-second exposure time. This speed did not allow me to conveniently decide and prepare the baths. Not only this, the negative must have been slightly coloured by the developer. The focus is not exactly on the Sun but rather on the body, obviously a more interesting topic on that occasion." [1]

Figure 3) **1908.** The Earliest British UFO Photograph? **(top right of opposite page):** Sept 14th 1908. Gosport, Hants. England.

Charles Fort mentions this image in his 1923 book *New Lands*:

"I have a datum that looks very much like the revelation of a ghost-moon, though I think of it myself in physical terms of light effects. In Country Queries and Notes (1:138,417), it is said that, in the sky of Gosport, Hampshire, night of Sept.14th 1908 was seen a light that came as if from an unseen moon. It may be that I can record that there was a moon-

like object in the sky of the Midlands and the south of England, this night, and that, though to human eyesight, this world, island of space, whatever it may have been, was invisible, it was, nevertheless, revealed. Upon this evening of Sept.14th 1908, David Packer, then in Northfield, Worcestershire saw a luminous appearance that he supposed was auroral, and photographed it. When the photograph was developed, it was seen that the 'auroral' light came from a large, moon-like object. A reproduction of the photograph is published in the English Mechanic (88,211). It shows an object as bright and as well developed as the conventionally accepted moon, but only to the camera had it revealed itself, and Mr Packer had caught upon film a space-island that had been made invisible to his eyes. It seems so, anyway." [2]

Figure 4) **1913 (below):**

This sighting occurred at 9.05 pm on 9th February 1913, from the Toronto Astronomical Observatory. The eminent astronomer Chant, together with other astronomers, noticed a strange body moving in the sky. Initially they sighted a shiny, deep red object travelling eastwards from the north and flying parallel to the skyline. Suddenly, other similar bodies appeared, all emanating from the same place and travelling in exactly the same direction as the one that had preceded them.

The astronomers could not believe their eyes. They moved in small groups of two, three or four, maintaining - this is most important- the same horizontal trajectory. When the astronomers lost sight of the bodies, they could hear a noise that sounded like distant thunder. The phenomenon lasted about three and a half minutes. After this sighting over Toronto, Canada, news came in relating to numerous identical sightings having taken place over a whole string of towns, going from Toronto all the way to Saint Roque Cape in Brazil. The bodies, as you may well see, seemed to have traced an 'arc' covering thousands of kilometers. The astronomers could then study the flight path followed by the enigmatic bodies. Eventually they came to the conclusion that *"it was a circular orbit, slant-*

ing over the equator in 50° 6', in a 90-minute period." In other words: those unknown bodies had managed to traverse around the whole planet Earth in an hour and a half. The term UFO - which stands for 'unidentified flying object'- did not exist at the time, so the witnesses called the 'flying bodies' 'Cyrilids', as they had appeared on Saint Cyril's day. The shooting star explanation proved weak, as they are only visible for a few seconds! [3]

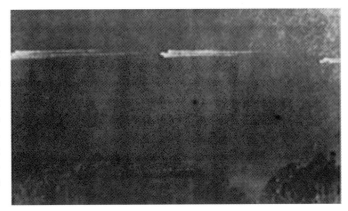

Figure 5 and 6) **1917 (*below and top of opposite page*):**
One of the themes running through this book is that certain religious events may have had a connection with UFOs. One such event from the 20th Century following these lines are the religious miracles at Fatima, Portugal in 1917. A series of events started on the 13th May,1917 when three young Portuguese children saw a white robed woman who asked them to return monthly to the same location for six months. On the second occasion, by word of mouth, fifty people turned up and heard an explosion followed by the sight of a cloud rising from a tree. On the third occasion, 4,500 people heard a buzzing noise, saw a cloud ascending from the same tree and heard an explosion. By September, 30,000 people had gathered expecting to witness miracles and sure enough they were not disappointed. Initially they saw a globe of light moving down the valley towards the three children and the air was described as being full of glistening bubbles as the object rose and disappeared into the sun. On the last occasion, on October 17th, 70,000 people were assembled. This time events were captured on camera. Initially, the heavy rain ceased. Then the clouds parted to reveal a silver coloured rotating disc, which emanated all the colours of the rainbow in succession. The disc suddenly plunged to the ground, throwing many people onto their knees in shock and awe. Then just as it appeared it was about to crash, it reversed and shot up into the sun. Following this, the crowd noticed their clothes and the ground they were standing on was dry. Luckily some photographs have emerged from this October day. The photograph (top right) is a very rare one which, shows the glowing object in the sky, photo 2 (below) shows many of the crowd looking up into the heavens at the phenomenon.

In today's context the events at Fatima sound like a classic UFO sighting. A revolving silvery disc, bright multicoloured lights, anomalous clouds! More amazingly 70,000 witnesses were present too and at least one cameraman. Of course back in 1917, the language of UFOs was unknown and generally across the globe it has been referred to as a case of a religious miracle rather than a UFO event.

© *Courtesy of*
Mr Wendelle Stevens

Figure 7) 1929 *(right)*:
Ward Sawmill, Ward, Colorado. April 1929. This incident is retold by the photographer's daughter:

"This photo was taken by my father Edward Pline at the sawmill in Ward where we lived at the time, I think it was 1929. I was about six years old then. My father was there to photograph the sawmill for some reason or another, and as he was taking the photo, he described a 'terrible thunderous bellow', and a large round thing as big as a very large boulder that moved through the air above them. You can see it in the picture. None of the sawmill workers saw the thing in the photo, but they all heard the sound and felt the ground shudder. Later in my life I tried researching the incident at the County Historical Society, but I did not find any references to it. My father passed on a few years after the incident, and I have not found any surviving sawmill workers from that time."Hetty Pline [4]

Figure 8) **Villa Uhlhorn, Germany, summer 1926** *(below)*:
A professional photographer photographing a family garden party, captured this UFO in the sky. This is Germany's oldest UFO photo.

© *Courtesy of Mr Wendelle Stevens*
UFO Photographs from Around the world published by Wendelle Stevens through his company UfO photo archives

Figure 9) **1937** *(below)*:
Leonard Lamoureux, aged 21 was on leave from the Army when he visited Vancouver City Hall to view and photograph the Christmas light display. Along with him was his brother Wilfred.

The two were suddenly astounded to see a 'bright blue light' drop straight down from the sky. It became larger as it did so and they were able to observe the source of the light as an object that Leonard described as 'two saucers' open ends facing each other, glowing bright blue. The object then moved 'dead straight' horizontally across the sky. When it just appeared to clear the flagpole on the roof of the City Hall, it came to an almost dead stop and Leonard clicked the shutter on the camera. The object then shot straight back up into the sky. *"They never had seen anything fly so fast!"* This scared them to death and they ran from the scene. The object made no sound.

Leonard's daughter, Debra DeCamillis who still lives in the Vancouver Lower Mainland area related this account to us. She remarked how vivid and excited her father sounded each time he described the sighting. Leonard Lamoureux passed away in 1992 and his brother Wilfred in 1955. Misfortune has it that the negative is no longer around, as some UFO researchers have suggested that this image is nothing but a watermark defect that appeared during the development of the print. Debra has this to add regarding this assertion:

"I know for fact there was no bubbles on the film, or watermarks because I was fascinated by negatives as a child and saw that negative many, many times. On the rest of the pictures there was nothing but pictures of lights, so I know it had no bubbles or watermarks on it." [5]

Deborah provided the following additional details:

"The camera was on a tri-pod of sorts because Dad was trying to take sequential shots of the courthouse to capture all the lights. But he was not using a timed exposure; his camera was not sophisticated enough. He did say that he could actually see the bubble or tail as he called it that the object was encapsulated in."

Figure 10) 1942 (below):
Tientsin, Hopeh Province, China. A young Japanese student Masujiro Kiryu, whilst going through his father's scrapbook of photographs from the China Campaign, just before World War II, discovered a strange cone-shaped object in the sky above a Tientsin Street. A number of people in the street are looking up and two are pointing up at the object. Apparently a sidewalk photographer snapped a picture of the strange machine and Kiryu's father bought it from the street vendor for a souvenir of the place.

© *Courtesy of Mr Wendle Stevens*

Figure 11) **1942. A negative from the LA Times of the event (above)**
This UFO was photographed on the 25th February 1942 and was featured in the
Los Angeles Times. A strange aerial intruder hovered over the Culver City area of
Los Angeles during that morning. It was described by one eyewitness, as 'enormous' and 'pale orange' in colour. Thinking it was a Japanese intruder the US
military launched a battery of artillery shells at the object. It seemed completely
oblivious to the hundreds of AA shells bursting on it, which caused it no evident
dismay. The blobs of light are not UFOs but bursts of anti-aircraft shells being
discharged (which totalled nearly 2000 rounds.) The beams of light are 'Earth-
based searchlights' focusing on the object, which can just be made out. The
attack on the aircraft lasted for half an hour before the object disappeared from
view.
When World War II finished the Los Angeles 'incident' was ratified by a military
document -kept secret for 30 years, which had been signed by the commander
in chief of the Allied Forces, general George C. Marshall, and sent to the president of the United States at the time, F. D. Roosevelt. This confidential report
declares that 1,430 rounds of ammunition were fired during the mysterious Los
Angeles air alarm. (General Marshall's document and ICUFON analysis). [6]

Figure 12) **1942** *(next page)*:
These luminous objects were sighted and photographed in the middle of a formation of Tachikawa Ki-36 reconnaissance planes in 1942. Numerous UFOs
were photographed during WW2. They received the nickname 'Foo Fighters'
from a maxim used by a cartoon comic character, Smokey Stover. This comic was
a favourite among US forces during WW2. The earliest accounts of foo-fighters
date back to 1940 and were seen throughout the war years. It was a worldwide

© Courtesy of the Fortean Picture Library

phenomenon with accounts from the European theatre, Norway, Germany, France, Sicily, The Pacific, Burma and Tunisia. Typically the objects were balls of light, usually orange and would appear from nowhere, tagging aircraft for up to 40 minutes.

Figure 13 & 14) **August 1945** *(opposite page right)*:
This remarkable photo of Mr LeMonde (pseudonym) was taken on a June morning in 1945 near the Pickwick Riding stables in Burbank, California. The exact date is not known. The photographer was the father of the subject in the photo, a motion picture producer with extensive technical experience. The object wasn't noticed until the photograph was developed. At the time, the term UFO or flying saucer didn't exist so the anomaly was assumed to be a speck of dust or an aeroplane. Therefore it is highly unlikely that this photograph was a hoax. I recently spoke to the photographer's son who told me that on the day of shooting the picture he and his father were on their way to their local riding stable called Pickwick Stables. Describing the event, the photographer's son said:

"Just as we got out on the trail that led through a park, which we often took in the past, we halted and he [his father] got down on the ground and using a fine German camera (Voightlander w/Carl Ziese lens) he aimed the camera up at me on the horse I was riding. He snapped the picture and mounted up and we rode off. Neither of us was aware of anything in the sky. I was looking at him and he was looking through the viewfinder

at me."

The photograph remained in the family album for more than 50 years. Upon the death of LeMonde's father, LeMonde went through the albums digitising the photos for family members.

It was then on enlargement that he noticed the strange craft (see detail top left.) It is to be noted that the clarity of the object indicates that this is not an item that had been thrown into the air. At the shutter speed listed, a thrown object would be slightly blurred. Some people have suggested the object is some kind of street light fixture. This idea was rejected for several reasons; researcher John Alexander says:

"Microscopic examination of the photo down to the gain level failed to reveal any suspending or supporting mechanisms. Further, behind the horse's neck, close to the saddle can be seen the curved arches of a sign that is over a drive-in movie theatre. That provides a reference for height. The object in question is well in the background behind the marquee. The distance infers that the object is much larger than a streetlight and substantially higher. Were it small and in the foreground, the supporting mechanism would be observable. It is not." [7]

Figure 15) 1946. Ghost Rockets *(right)*:
This UFO was photographed by Erik Reuterswürd at 2.30 PM on July 9th, 1946. As it was a sunny summer day, there were many witnesss. Reuterswürd happened to snap the picture by chance from an air watchtower close to Guldsmedshyttan in mid-Sweden. Throughout the year, numerous 'ghost rockets' were reported flying over Norway and Sweden, and even crashing. This is one of the few known photographs of the phenomenon. Ufologist Tim Good in his 1987 book *Above Top Secret*, commented on the ghost rockets:

"In 1946 the Scandinavian countries reported over 2,000 unidentified flying objects over their airspace. These objects usually looked like rockets with fiery exhausts, and they sometimes performed unusual maneuvers as they passed overhead. At first they were thought to be captured German V-2 missiles that were being tested by the Russians, but British radar experts said they did not come from the U.S.S.R. Experts said that 80% of the reports were due to natural phenomena such as meteors, but they had no explanation for the other 20%. Oddly, the objects appeared over some of the southern European countries also, such as Greece, where an official investigation was conducted in 1947. The leader of that investigation, Professor Paul Santorini, revealed in 1967 that their investigation showed that the objects were not missiles. He also said that before they could proceed any further, the army ordered the investigation stopped. Even today, fifty years later, official files on the ghost rockets are still classified documents. " [8]

SOURCES

1) The Zacatecas sighting is mentioned in *The Flying Saucer Story* by Trench, B (1966). Ace Books Inc, New York and *Operation Trojan Horse* by J Keel (1973) Sphere Books, London. Interestingly the author recently received correspondence from the great-great grandson of Jose Bonilla after viewing the photograph on the author's website *www.ufoartwork.com.*

2) Footnote : *New Lands* by Charles Fort Boni & Liveright. New York 1923
Published online at *http://www.sacred-texts.com/fort/lands/*

3) *Courtesy of the Spanish UFO Investigator & writer JJ Benitez*

4) Thanks to researcher Alain Stauffer of Geneva for supplying me with the photo and information.

5) Thanks to Martin Jasek of *www.ufobc.ca* for this information and photographs.

6) Military Archives Division Gen. George C. Marshall, Chief of Staff brief. *Memorandum on February 26,* to President Franklin D. Roosevelt about the "mysterious" Los Angeles air alarm. *Copy of original transcript below:*

MEMORANDUM FOR THE PRESIDENT:

The following is the information we have from GHQ at this moment regarding the air alarm over Los Angeles of yesterday morning:

From details available at this hour:

1. *Unidentified airplanes, other than American Army or Navy planes, were probably over Los Angeles, and were fired on by elements of the 37th CA Brigade (AA) between 3:12 and 4:15 AM. These units expended 1430 rounds of ammunition.*
2. *As many as fifteen airplanes may have been involved, flying at various speeds from what is officially reported as being 'very low' to as much as 200 MPH and at elevations from 9000 to 18000 feet.*
3. *No bombs were dropped.*
4. *No casualties among our troops.*
5. *No planes were shot down.*
6. *No American or Navy planes were in action.*

Investigation continuing.

It seems reasonable to conclude that if unidentified airplanes were involved they may have been from commercial sources, operated by enemy agents for purposes of spreading alarm, disclosing location of anti-aircraft positions, and slowing production through blackout. Such conclusion is supported by varying speed of operation and the fact that no bombs were dropped.

(Sgd) G. C. MARSHALL - Chief of Staff

---

7) John Alexander is a member of the Science Advisory Board of The National Institute for Discovery Science (NIDS). This is a privately funded, private sector research organisation focusing on empirical and hypothesis-based scientific exploration of aerial phenomena that expand conventional knowledge. NIDS is particularly interested in phenomena that appear to be under intelligent guidance and in the possible habitation of space by intelligent life.

8) *Above Top Secret* by Timothy Good Sidgewick and Jackson 1987. Timothy Good has written several excellent titles on the UFO phenomenon and this was his first.

CONCLUSION

CONCLUSION
CONCLUSION

We have now come to the end of our journey into the past. Many of the myths we read in the third chapter appear to describe visitations from the stars. We have examined historical artwork depicting UFOs and read a series of historical recorded sightings. We have looked at a collection of unusual artifacts, such as the fabulous Mitchell Hedges Crystal Skull and we have examined ancient maps, whose source maps date from an even older epoch depicting ice-free Antarctica.

I feel the information in this book represents a strong case for the visitation of ETs throughout history. If we accept this and take on board the fact that the UFO phenomenon is still with us today, this raises some profound questions. Who are piloting these craft? Maybe they are earthlings time-travelling from the future? Why are they visiting us? Will we meet these visitors? Once we have these answers we may come closer to those age old questions that have haunted man for many millennia: who are we? Where do we come from? And where are we going?

Despite all this evidence there is little interest from the academic community. Ufology is a sensitive subject within academic circles. It is still considered a fringe or lunatic subject by many. Professor John Mack from Harvard Medical School encountered problems with his University hierarchy when he made public his interest in Alien Abductions. A number of academics privately express an interest in Ufology, but they risk their reputation or at worst their job, if they openly express their opinions. There is also no cohesion between the differing fields of academia; the anthropologist possesses knowledge of ancient cave paintings, the museum curator has strange artifacts under his ownership. The resulting lack of communication between these groups makes it difficult for the earnest researcher to identify common threads.

Many who have looked at the subject of ETs, have concluded there is a cover-up by the government and intelligence agencies of the world. A number of plausible reasons have been put forward:

THE IMPACT ON RELIGION.
Maybe the biblical God was an ET and if Jesus didn't die for our sins, this puts the whole construct of Christianity off balance.

THE IMPACT ON PEOPLE IN GENERAL

It has been theorised that many would not be able to carry on with their lives. Some would want to worship ETs as Gods, some would panic and perceive them as a threat, whilst others would want them to solve the world's problems. This may lead to a regression in our progress and development as a species. Historically, when an advanced civilisation meets a lesser civilisation the latter is absorbed and disappears, for example, the Spanish lead by Pizarro conquered the Incas and they consequently vanished from existence.

THE IMPACT ON POWER STRUCTURES.

If it was shown that ETs were real, people may want to seek their wisdom and guidance and as a consequence ignore traditional governmental power structures.

THE IMPACT ON THE WORLD'S ECONOMY AND OIL INDUSTRY.

If the ETs use revolutionary clean, hyper efficient propulsion systems, society may want to utilise them as a replacement for our existing power generation. This would have a direct impact on the oil industry, which is the backbone of the world economy.

THE POSSIBILITY OF A SUPER WEAPON.

The undoubted high technology behind these craft could be turned into advanced weaponry if it got into the wrong hands and could lead to disaster.

For some, particularly those who wish the status quo to remain, these reasons form quite a convincing argument for an ET cover-up. Possibly the time has now come for the truth to be told.

The idea of ETs visiting our planet for millennia is a paradigm that not everyone accepts or feels comfortable with. If the day came when we all became aware of ETs, we would collectively experience a shattering of our worldview and consequently a new paradigm would replace the old.
Our spiritually inert, egocentric civilisation would have to mature and realise its place in the universe. If ETs did return publicly maybe they will not want us to worship them as 'gods' as man may have done in ancient times. Assuming we do not destroy our planet through wars or pollution, we may be now entering the epoch (as the Mayans predicted) and now a hand is being offered to us, can we take that step?[1]

Every epoch produces individuals who shatter the existing paradigm. Copernicus was one. He postulated the Sun was at the centre of the solar system. Each of these farsighted personalities faces strong opposition and are often considered cranks. This has happened throughout history. Today, those researchers in Ufology are in the same situation. Perhaps one day they will be vindicated.

I will leave you with a quote from Paracelsus from his 15th Century treatise entitled *Why these Beings Appear to Us*. He says:

"Everything God creates manifests itself to Man sooner or later. Sometimes God confronts him with the devil and the spirits in order to convince him of their existence. From the top of heaven he also sends the Angels, his servants. Thus these beings appear to us, not in order to stay among us or become allied with us, but in order for us to become able to understand them. These apparitions are scarce, to tell the truth. But why should it be otherwise? Is it not enough for one to see an Angel, in order for all of us to believe in the other Angels?"

SOURCES

1) For more information about the Mayan prophecies and their like from around the 'ancient world' see the works of John Major Jenkins, *Cosmogenesis 2012, published by Bear and Company,* and Neil Hague's book *Through Ancient Eyes,* also published by Quester.

BIBLIOGRAPHY

Alford, Alan; *Gods of the New Millennium*. Hodder and Staughton 1998

Baval, Richard and **Hancock**, Graham; *Keeper of Genesis*. William Heinmann, London 1996

Bonechi; *All of Egypt*. Bonechi Publishing House

Bramley, William; *Gods of Eden*. Avon, New York 1993

Childers, Ian;*The Concise Oxford Dictionary of Art and Artists* OUP1900, 1996

Childress, David Hatcher; *The Anti-Gravity Handbook*. Adventures Unlimted Press 1990

Downing, Barry H; *The Bible and Flying Saucers*. Sphere Books 1969

Drake, W Raymond; *Gods and Spaceman in the Ancient East*. Sphere 1973

European Painting (in Russian). 1999. Moscow, Russia.

Feats and Wisdom of the Ancients. Time Life Books

Flying Saucer Review Magazine. FSR Publications Ltd

Fort, Charles; *New Lands*. Boni & Liveright. New York 1923

Fuller, John G; *The Interrupted Journey*. 1966. Dell Pub. Co

Good, Timothy; *Beyond Top Secret*. Sidgwick and Jackson, London 1996

Good, Timothy; *Alien Base*. Century, London 1998

Good, Timothy; *Unearthly Disclosure*. Century, London 2000

Good, Timothy; *Above Top Secret*. Sidgwick and Jackson 1987

Goring, Rosemary; *Dictionary of Beliefs and Religions* edited by, Wordsworth Editions, 1995

Green, Vaughn M; *The Six-Thousand-Year-Old Spacesuit*. Merlin Engine Works 1982

Hancock, Graham ; *Fingerprints of the Gods*. William Heinmann, London 1995

Hapgood, Dr. Charles; *Maps of the Ancient Sea Kings; Evidence of Advanced Civilization in the Ice Age*. Chilton Books.Philadelphia and New York 1966.

Hobana, Ion & Weverbergh, Julien; *UFO's From Behind The Iron Curtain*. Bantam Books 1972

Huyghe, Patrick; *The Field Guide to Extraterrestrials*. New English Library 1997

Icke, David; *The Robots Rebellion*. Gateway Books. Bath 1994

Janson, Anthony F (edited by); *History of Art*. Thames and Hudson, London 1995

Leakey, Mary; *Africa's; Vanishing Art*. Doubleday 1983

Levine, Robert *A Thirteenth-Century Life of Charlemagne (volume III of Viard's edition of the Grandes Chroniques)* translated by published by Garland Press, 1991

Lewels, Joe, Ph. D; *The Reptilians: Humanity's Historical Link to the Serpent Race*. Fate Magazine July 1996

Lt. Grey; *Journals of Two Expeditions of Discovery in Northwest and Western Australia 1837, 1838, & 1839* - London, T. and W. Boone 1841

Lycosthenes, Conrad ; *Prodigiorum Ac Ostentorum Chronicon*

Mack, Dr. J; *Passport to the Cosmos*. Thorsons, London 2000

Magor, John; *Our UFO Visitors*. Hancock House 1977

Marrs, Jim; *Alien Agenda.* Harper Collins, 1997

Menier, Pierre; Discours Espouventable. *Des Signes Qui Sont Apparus sur la mer de Gennes,* 1608

Mysteries of the Unexplained, Reader's Digest Association, February 1985

Notiziairo UFO no. 8 Sept/Oct 1996

Noyes, Ralph; *The Crop Circle Enigma.* Gateway Books 1990

Pinotti, Dr Roberto; *Indo-Aryan Traditions and History of Astronautics.* Oct 8-15 1988

Plot, Professor R; *The Natural History of Staffordshire.* 1686

Shuker, Dr Karl P N;*The Unexplained.* Carlton Books 1996

Story, Ronald; *The Space Gods Revealed.* New English Library 1976

Strieber, Whitley, *Communion.* Avon 1988

Strieber, Whitley; *Hidden Agendas series UFO Briefing Document* Dell Publishing Company 2000

Sunday Times Magazine 15th September 2002 *Times Newspapers Ltd*

The Holy Bible - King James Authorised Ed.

Thompson, Richard, *Alien Identities.* Govardhan Hill, California 1993

Vallee, Jacques, *Passport to Magonia.* Tandem Publishing 1975

Vallee, Jacques; *UFO's in Space: Anatomy of a Phenomenon.* Ballantine Books 1965

Von Däniken , Erich; *Chariots of the Gods.* Souvenir Press 1969

Von Däniken, Erich; *According to the Evidence.* Souvenir Press 1977

Von Däniken, Erich; *Gold of the Gods.* Souvenir Press 1973

Von Däniken, Erich; *Return of the Gods.* Element Books 1997

Von Däniken, Erich; *Arrival of the Gods.* Element Books 1998

Walters, Ed and Frances; *UFO's The Gulf Breeze Sightings.* Bantam Press, London 1990

Wendelle Stevens; *UFO Contact from the Pleiadies, a supplementary report.* Arizona USA 1990

Wilson, Colin; *Alien Dawn.* Virgin, London 1998

Wundram, Manfred ; *Painting of the Renaissance.* 1997 Benedikt Taschen Verlag

X Factor Magazine. An eight-volume magazine on the unexplained published between 1995-1999 by Marshall Cavendish Ltd. 119 Wardour Street,London W1V 3TD.

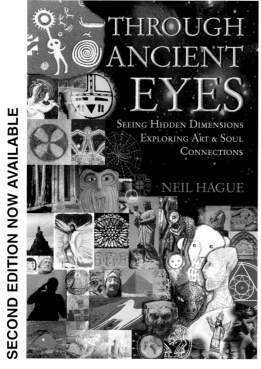

SECOND EDITION NOW AVAILABLE

PUBLISHED IN NOVEMBER 2004

ISBN 0-9541904-0-8 £16 $25
1233mm x 156mm 288 Pages

Through Ancient Eyes explores how art is a metaphysi-
cal activity, while illustrating the art and soul connections that have existed since ancient times. Drawing
on a wealth of information, which includes prehistoric
art and prophecy, through to the work of William
Blake – this fascinating book unlocks ancient wisdom
that has inspired artists from all ages.

Expanding our view of the creative process,
we are taken on a journey that weaves together a
cornucopia of myths, archetypes and symbols,
which through art,
can reveal hidden dimensions of the soul.

*"Through Ancient Eyes is an essential read for anyone
interested in the power of the imagination, and how art and
nature can transport us
into different levels of awareness. "*
Jaye Beldo
Author of the *Dream Nation Workshops*

ISBN 0-9541904-2-4 £18 $30
233mm x 156mm 300pages (with colour plates)

Journeys in the Dreamtime explores the 'illusion of
time' and the ancient myths that encapsulate stories
of interdimensional forces, hidden worlds and the
sacred places – as understood by Earth's greatest
visionaries. All religions, 'inspired art movements'
including the movie-blockbusters we flock to today,
are littered with archetypal symbols, legendary stories of good against evil and imagery associated
with 'other worlds'. From the legends of the
Dreamtime to the concept of the *Matrix*, this book
takes us on a journey into the timeless realms of the
imagination. Get ready for a roller-coaster ride into
the deepest recesses of the mind as Neil Hague
explores the past, present and future, symbols,
superheroes and the stars systems that have inspired
humanity since the beginning of time.

*"Neil Hague's work is unique - the language of an open
and highly creative mind. You look with your eyes, but he
speaks to your heart."*
David Icke

AVAILABLE AT ALL GOOD BOOKSTORES

To order these titles in the USA
visit *www.hiddenmysteries.com*
Hidden Mysteries 22241 Pinedale Lane
Frankston, Texas 75763
Telephone: 903-876-3256

Quester

To order these titles in the UK
visit *www.questerpublications.com*
or; *www.btinternet.com/~www.seeing*
P.O. Box 3226, Chester CH4 7ZB
Telephone: +44 (0) 1244 680949